Penguin Books
Your Mortgage

Clifford German was born in Northampton
in 1934 and educated at the local grammar
school. He was commissioned in the Navy
and qualified as a Russian interpreter. After
obtaining a first in geography at St John's
College, Cambridge, where he was also
president of the University Liberal Club,
he taught geography at the University of
Michigan and at Wayne State University,
Detroit, and co-wrote, with John Cole,
Economic Geography of the Soviet Union
(1961). He wrote for the *Financial Times* and
The Times before joining the *Daily Telegraph*
in 1966, becoming Financial Correspondent
in 1968 and, later, Associate City Editor. In
1986 he became City Editor of *Today*, and he
is now City Editor of *The Scotsman*.

Norwich Union is unique among Britain's
major financial institutions. Its parent company, the Norwich Union Life Insurance
Society, is a mutual life office which distri-
butes all its profits to the policy-holders and
not to shareholders.

The group offers a wide range of financial
services – not only insurance cover for
people and property but also endowment
mortgage policies, pensions and other
investment plans – with the stated aim of
providing best value for money to present
and future life policy-holders. The assets of
the Norwich Union group amount to well
over £10,000 million.

Your Mortgage
The Norwich Union Guide

Clifford German

Penguin Books

PENGUIN BOOKS

Published by the Penguin Group
27 Wrights Lane, London W8 5TZ, England
Viking Penguin Inc., 40 West 23rd Street, New York, New York 10010, USA
Penguin Books Australia Ltd, Ringwood, Victoria, Australia
Penguin Books Canada Ltd, 2801 John Street, Markham, Ontario, Canada LR3 1B4
Penguin Books (NZ) Ltd, 182–190 Wairau Road, Auckland 10, New Zealand

Penguin Books Ltd, Registered Offices: Harmondsworth, Middlesex, England

First published 1988

Typeset by Fox + Partners, Bath, and PCS, Frome

Made and printed in Great Britain by Richard Clay Ltd, Bungay

Contents

List of tables

List of figures

Acknowledgements

I would like to thank everyone who helped in the writing of this book, including Adrian Coles and Tricia McLaughlin of the Building Societies Association, Mike Sismey, Steve Perry, Alan Hawkins and Barry Bissett of the Nationwide Anglia building society, Andrew Whybrow of the Halifax, David Wragg and John Jennings-Chick of the Bristol & West, Rhiddian Jones and Norman Evans of Lloyds bank, Tim Orbell of Black Horse Agencies, Peter Seymour and John Wilson of the National Westminster bank, Gil Gillis of Natwest Home Loans Ltd, Richard Lacy of National Home Loans Corporation, Mike Parris of the Household Mortgage Corporation, Charles Wishart of John Charcol, Vincent Connolly of Pointon York, Roger Stanley of Prudential Property Services, Ken Hurst, Terry Smith and Gerry Uren of Norwich Union, Ian Brown of the Housing Corporation, Stephen Quirke of the *Mortgage Magazine* and, last but not least, Philip Coggan of the *Financial Times*, who introduced me to the project, Chris Walker of the *Financial Times*, who drew the maps and charts, and Muriel German, who made the word processor work when I could not.

The opinions expressed in this book are my own and not those of Norwich Union, who, while supporting this book wholeheartedly, have given me complete freedom in writing it.

Introduction

Mortgages are no longer simply available. They are being marketed with all the enthusiasm and advertising hype which a few years ago was reserved for soap powder and hair shampoo. Instead of waiting weeks for a building society to decide whether to grant a plain grey mortgage loan, today's borrower faces an army of salesmen eager to sell a whole range of 'designer' mortgage packages, tailored to individual needs.

The mortgage market has changed out of all recognition in the last few years. Most local councils have been forced to stop lending money to local residents to help them buy houses. But at the same time the government has deliberately stimulated competition for the building societies, who used to have the field almost entirely to themselves, and made the mortgage market much more commercial. The big British banks – National Westminster, Barclays, Lloyds and Midland, the TSB and the Scottish banks – have been encouraged to move into the home loans business. They have been followed by dozens of foreign banks. More recently, special mortgage companies have been set up.

Building societies have been forced to compete with each other as well as with the new lenders. Dozens of societies have sought safety in mergers, or have been taken over by bigger competitors. The societies that remain are being allowed to offer new services, and the top half dozen have started buying up estate agents with the aim of selling mortgages, insurance and houses all in the same package. But competition has become so fierce that by the summer of 1987 the societies' share of the mortgage business had fallen to a bare 50 per cent.

Mortgages themselves have also changed. Traditional repayment mortgages (which borrowers repay in monthly instalments of capital and interest combined) have been overtaken in popularity by insurance-linked mortgages, where borrowers pay interest and also put money into an insurance policy. At the end of its term, the insurance policy pays off the mortgage and, if all goes well, provides a tax-free bonus as well.

But the choice faced by borrowers is growing wider still. It includes a combined mortgage and pension plan; a mortgage combined with investment in unit trusts; and special low-start mortgages which allow young home buyers to borrow more than they could afford on a conventional mortgage basis, by making low repayments at first and higher ones in later years when (the theory is) they can better afford it. Estate agents, insurance brokers, insurance companies and financial advisers are all busy earning commission by selling mortgages on behalf of banks and building societies, insurance companies and mortgage companies.

With so many lenders competing to provide mortgages, the government no longer tries to stop people increasing their mortgages to raise money to spend on things other than housing, or remortgaging their homes and moving from one lender to another without moving house. The result has been an explosion of mortgage lending and a boom in property prices, although the experts are still arguing about whether this is a consequence or a coincidence. The level of new lending has more than trebled in six years, and more than two million new loans are made each year, including half a million further advances to existing borrowers.

Property prices have soared to record levels, outpacing inflation and even incomes in recent years. Many first-time buyers have had to share properties with friends to get on to the housing ladder at all. In London the average house costs well over five years' average income, and ordinary families moving from other parts of the country stand little chance of finding a home they can afford to buy. But eight million borrowers are not complaining. They still get tax relief on the interest they pay on the first £30,000 of their loans, and their homes are the best investments they ever made.

1
Bricks and mortar – the best investment?

Britain has become a nation of home owners largely over the past 40 years. At the end of World War II in 1945, only one family in four owned their own home; one in five lived in a council house and well over half still rented homes owned by private landlords. Since then the changes have been rapid, and owner-occupied housing has emerged as the most important sector of the housing market, decisively outgrowing both council housing and the private rented sector.

Between 1945 and 1970, home ownership and council housing both grew steadily in importance while the private rented sector dwindled. The proportion of families who owned their own homes or were in the process of buying them grew gradually to 29 per cent in 1950, accelerated to 42 per cent by 1960, and reached 50 per cent in 1970. By then the council housing sector had expanded to 30 per cent and the private rented sector had shrunk to under 20 per cent.

Since 1970 council housing has been hamstrung by shortages of cash for building and by the policy of selling council homes to sitting tenants – a policy first proposed by the Conservatives under Edward Heath, tentatively introduced by the Labour Party in 1975 and then enthusiastically endorsed and expanded by the Conservatives under Margaret Thatcher.

Reinforced by council house sales, the owner-occupiers have gone on to become a clear majority, accounting for 60 per cent of all households in 1984 and still advancing at a rate of a little over one per cent a year. Council housing peaked at 32 per cent of all households in 1977 and has since fallen back to little more than 25 per cent, while the private rented sector has continued to decline, down to fewer than 10 per cent of all households.

The transformation has been financed by a massive amount of mortgage finance provided by building societies, banks and (most recently) by specialized mortgage companies – all at very competitive rates. It has been encouraged by special tax concessions: mortgage interest up to a certain level can be paid out of untaxed income, and there is no capital gains tax to pay on owner-occupied homes, however expensive they are and however much they may have gained in value.

Every major political party now enthusiastically supports wider home ownership and sings the praises of a property-owning democracy. The abolition of tax relief on mortgage interest, which reduces the cost of borrowing to buy a home, is now politically unthinkable for any government – although within all parties there is pressure for restrictions (see Chapter 3).

Home ownership has brought about enormous social changes, encouraging families to save and manage money. The monthly mortgage payment has become the most important element in the budget of most young couples. Roughly 20 per cent of all new mortgage loans each year have been going to help borrowers under the age of 25 to buy their own home, and one person in three in Britain now has a mortgage by the time they are 25 years old, making Britons the youngest home owners in Europe and probably in the world.

Homes as an investment

Bricks and mortar have turned out to be the best long-term investment the average family could make. Unlike shares, houses earn no income, but home owners live rent-free, and pay no tax on the benefits they enjoy. With tax relief on mortgage interest, it is almost as cheap to buy property with borrowed money as it would be to rent it – even if rented properties were easily available, which in most parts of the country they are not. Mortgage interest rates have tended to rise, but in most years interest costs have not even kept pace with rising property values. In the last ten years alone, most families have seen the value of their houses treble.

Home ownership has made it possible for families to build up some capital for the first time in their lives, and during the 1950s, 1960s and 1970s it helped to make the distribution of wealth less unequal. Over short periods, share prices have risen faster than house prices. But over most of the last 20 or 30 years, houses as an investment have easily outperformed stocks and shares, and other alternatives such as gold, stamps and antiques.

House prices are also much less volatile than the values of other investments. Share prices on the London stock market have regularly doubled or trebled only to be halved again (see Figure 1), and individual shares have fluctuated even more. The price of gold rose steadily in the 1970s and then fell for most of the 1980s. Art and antiques have also suffered from changing fashions which have pushed prices up and then down again.

Property prices

The average home in Great Britain cost about £2,000 in 1950, rising to about £2,400 by 1960 and £5,000 by 1970. Since then increases have been remarkably rapid, and the average home had risen to £12,000 by 1975, £24,000 in 1980 and £48,000 in 1987, an increase of roughly 20 times over a period when the cost of living as a whole has risen about tenfold.

During the 1950s, property prices rose at a rate of about 2 per cent a year, which was slightly below the rate of inflation. But since 1959 house prices have risen approximately twice as fast as the cost of living generally. During the 1960s property prices rose by about 7 per cent a year, which was roughly twice as fast as prices in the economy as a whole. Since then house prices have continued to rise by an average of about 15 per cent a year – still well above the inflation rate – but the rate of increase has varied much more widely.

There have been three spectacular surges in house prices: in 1972–73, in 1978–80 and again in 1986–88. Between these surges, prices have continued to rise, but much more slowly. The first surge began in the second half of 1971, and over the next two years the price of the average house almost doubled, from about £6,000 to £11,000. At the very peak of the boom, during the second half of 1972, prices were rising at an average rate of more than 40 per cent a year.

By the second half of 1973, prices were rising much more slowly – and in the mid-1970s, they failed to keep pace with inflation. But early in 1978 prices began to take off again; over the next two and a half years, the average price of homes went up from about £14,000 to around £24,000, and the annual rate of increase reached 30 per cent during 1979. The boom collapsed again in the second half of 1980, and the property market was flat in 1981 and 1982, although inflation remained a serious problem.

The third property boom was less spectacular, but prices rose by about 15 per cent a year on average in 1986 and 1987, and the average price in Britain went up from about £33,000 in 1985 to almost £50,000 by the end of 1987.

Property prices have fallen at certain times in certain districts. Prices of luxury homes in central London fell in 1981, for example, as a result of the slump in Middle East oil revenues and a sharp rise in the value of the pound against the dollar – trends which reduced the demand for such properties among wealthy Middle Eastern and American buyers.

House prices have also fallen in response to local problems.

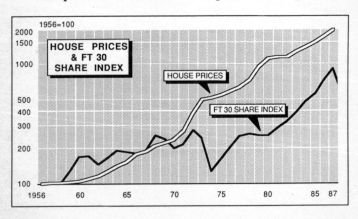

Figure 1
House prices have risen faster and more consistently than the 30-share index, even before shares fell sharply in the autumn of 1987.

Prices fell in Northern Ireland in 1981 as a result of both the general recession and the local political situation, and have since lagged far behind prices in the rest of Britain. Property prices in the Aberdeen area were badly hit by the slump in oil prices and the sharp decline in exploration and drilling in the North Sea during 1985. During the year-long pit strike in 1985–86, property in South Wales and West Yorkshire became virtually impossible to sell. But house prices have not fallen throughout the whole country in any year since 1954.

Property and inflation

Over the long term, property prices have comfortably kept ahead of inflation. According to the Nationwide Anglia building society, they rose faster than prices in general in 27 of the 33 years from 1954 to 1986; they failed to do so from 1974 to 1977 and again in 1980 and 1981 – the periods between the three recent surges in house prices when they clearly outpaced inflation.

Between the middle of 1971 and the third quarter of 1973, the real price of property (that is, the price after allowing for inflation) rose by a staggering 50 per cent in less than two and a half years. Then, in the years 1974 to 1977 most of the gains

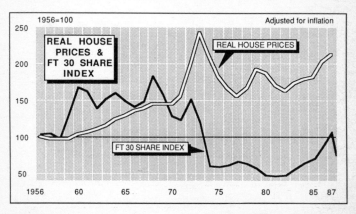

Figure 2
Allowing for inflation makes three recent surges in house prices clear — and highlights the poor performance of shares in the 1970s.

of the previous two years were eroded away. From the middle of 1977 to the end of 1979, however, prices rose 30 per cent in real terms. Half those gains were lost again in 1980 and 1981. But each surge in prices started from a higher point, and prices again began to outperform inflation in 1983. Property prices then began to climb steadily ahead of inflation, bringing real prices close to record levels again in 1987 (see Figure 2).

Property prices doubled in real terms between 1960 and 1987. In some years, home owners have made more profit on the value of their home than they have earned by going to work. And, unlike income, the capital gain on their main home is tax-free. Home owners have to live somewhere of course – so the gain in value is of only academic interest to some people. But property is an asset which can be used as security for a loan or to generate a lump sum when home owners retire or want to move to a less expensive home, and forms a valuable inheritance for their families.

Types of property

Some types of property have appreciated faster than others. The price of new houses is generally higher than average, but over the years the difference between new and old house prices has varied from as little as 5 per cent to as much as 20 per cent. It depends on the price of building land, and the size and style of property being built at the time. New house prices rose

Table 1
Price increases of different types of property

Percentage price increase, 1983–87

Date of building:	Pre 1919	1920–45	1946–60	1961–80	New	All
Terraced/town houses	75	94	61	66	79	77
Semi-detached houses	67	60	53	52	45	57
Detached houses	59	59	60	52	47	52
Bungalows	30	61	54	50	37	50
Flats and maisonettes	97	96	68	70	88	86
All properties	72	62	48	53	56	59

Source Halifax Building Society, 1987

more slowly than average house prices between 1960 and 1975. In the late 1970s, new house prices went up faster than average, but in the last few years older houses have again risen faster (see Table 1).

The price of older houses (built before 1919) is still generally below average, but the difference has narrowed from about 15 per cent below average in the 1950s and 1960s to about 10 per cent in the 1970s and 1980s. This is partly because the decline in house building has increased demand for older houses, and partly because the fashion has changed from demolishing them to renovating them.

Gentrification

The swing back to renovating rather than rebuilding also means that most new homes are now being built in suburban and small-town areas or relegated to less convenient sites, where land values are often lower than in older residential suburbs. Rises in travel costs and increasing real incomes have also encouraged the 'gentrification' of older suburbs and pushed up the price of older houses. They tend to be in districts which are closer to city centres, where commuting to work is quicker and cheaper, while a new generation of wealthier buyers can appreciate the period charms of older homes and also afford to renovate them.

In the last few years, prices of homes built before 1919 have shown the biggest increases. Properties built between the two World Wars have risen in price more slowly than pre-1919 properties, but they too have risen faster than new homes. The slowest increases have been in homes built in the 1940s and 1950s, presumably because they offer neither the prime positions and the period charm of Georgian, Victorian and Edwardian homes nor the standard amenities (such as central heating and modern kitchens and bathrooms) which are now built into new homes.

The prices of flats and maisonettes, terraced homes and town houses have also risen faster than the prices of traditional semi-detached and detached homes and the bungalows which used to be every suburban home owner's dream. Bungalows in particular are very much out of fashion. But it is a matter of convenience and accessibility as well as taste. Flats in property built before 1919 have shown the fastest increases of all, presumably because they are in areas which had the biggest scope for improvements. Terraced homes built before 1919 have also kept pace with the price of new town houses, and have comfortably beaten modern terraces.

Detached and semi-detached houses and bungalows of all ages appear to have appreciated more slowly than either flats or town houses. That may well be because they need more valuable space than flats and town houses, and are increasingly being built in the outer suburbs, small towns and the country-side, where prices are lower.

Council house sales

More than a million flats and houses formerly owned by local councils have been sold to sitting tenants since 1980 as a result of the Conservative government's policy of privatizing state and local authority assets, in order both to increase government revenue and to cut government and local authority spending and borrowing. They form a distinct new section of the property market.

Price trends in former council houses and flats are difficult to monitor because all council-owned homes have been offered to sitting tenants at substantial discounts (which vary according to how long the tenants have lived there). Initially, tenants who sold their house within five years of buying it had to repay part of the discount. The limit has now been reduced to three years, and a steady trickle of former council houses is now coming on to the market. But the small number of homes which have so far come up for resale still seem to sell for rather less than similar properties in nearby areas, probably because former council properties still carry a social stigma, especially on estates where most homes are still council-owned.

Regional differences

Prices of similar homes in different parts of the country vary widely, and the differences have increased sharply in the last few years as the north-south prosperity gap has widened (see

Figures 3 and 4). At the peak of the 1986–88 price boom, in London the average house price was nearly £70,000 – a record 60 per cent above the national average, followed by south-east England with prices 40 per cent above the national average.

Prices were also above the national average in both south-west England and East Anglia. In every other part of the country prices were well below the average, ranging from about 20 per cent below in the east and west Midlands and in Scotland, to 25 per cent below in Wales and north-west England and 30 per cent below in Northern Ireland, northern England, and Yorkshire & Humberside.

Prices in London were then roughly twice as high as in the rest of the country and 2.5 times as high as in the north of England; the same money would buy a one-bedroom flat in London or a modern four-bedroom house north of the Trent.

The north-south divide

The gap between north and south is nothing new – property has always been more expensive in the London area. But the differences have varied considerably over the past two decades. Prices in London and southern England are the most dynamic, but they are also the most volatile. They accelerate fastest when the economy as a whole is prosperous and the housing market is buoyant, while prices in other regions grow more sedately. In a recession, prices in London and the south-east slow down and other parts of the country begin to catch up.

In 1970, when house prices first started rising strongly, property in London cost 40 per cent more than the national average and in the south-east 25 per cent more. Scotland and south-west England were close to the national average, with the rest of the country straggling behind. The cheapest houses were in Yorkshire & Humberside, where they cost 73 per cent of the national average and just over half the London average.

London prices spurted ahead in the first house-price boom and were 50 per cent above the national average in 1972, only to slip back to a low of just 23 per cent above the national average in 1976–78, as prices in other parts of the country caught up.

After 1978, London, the south-east, the south-west and East

Anglia began moving ahead of the rest of the country again – gradually at first – while Wales, Scotland and northern England began falling behind again. Prices in London rose to 30 per cent above the national average in the second house-price boom (in 1980), and slipped back again to 27 per cent above average as it came to an end in 1981. But in 1982, prices in London were again 30 per cent above the average and then began accelerating rapidly, followed by the south-east, the south-west, East Anglia and east Midlands. By 1987, the gap between north and south was wider than ever.

Over the whole period between 1970 and 1987, house prices in the United Kingdom rose eightfold. But prices in London rose more than nine times, and in the south-east, the south-west and East Anglia, rises were well above the national average. Prices in the east Midlands have kept pace with the national average, while Yorkshire & Humberside and the west Midlands have seen rises just below the average, but property prices in the north and north-west, Wales, Scotland and Northern Ireland all grew less than sevenfold – much more slowly than the average.

The slowest increases of all have been in Scotland, where the

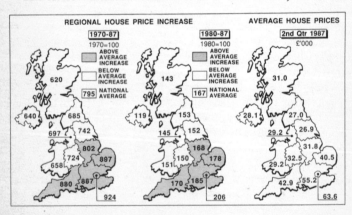

Figure 3
House prices rose eightfold between 1970 and 1987, and by 67 per cent between 1980 and 1987. The south has consistently beaten the north, and is now more expensive by a factor of two or more.

The maps and tables use the standard planning regions:
1 London (the old GLC area)
2 South-east England (Essex, Kent, Surrey, Sussex, Hampshire, Berkshire, Oxfordshire, Buckinghamshire, Hertfordshire and Bedfordshire)
3 East Anglia (Norfolk, Suffolk and Cambridgeshire)
4 South-west England (Cornwall, Devon, Somerset, Avon, Gloucestershire, Wiltshire and Dorset)
5 East Midlands (Northamptonshire, Leicestershire, Derby, Nottinghamshire and Lincolnshire)
6 West Midlands (Warwickshire, West Midlands Conurbation, Hereford & Worcester, Shropshire and Staffordshire)
7 North-west England (Lancashire, Cheshire, Merseyside and Manchester)
8 Yorkshire & Humberside
9 Northern England (Cumbria, Northumberland, Tyne & Wear, Durham and Cleveland)
10 Wales
11 Scotland
12 Northern Ireland

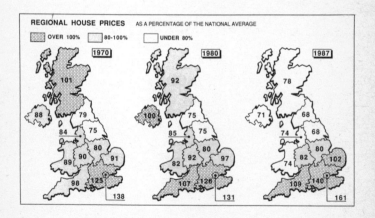

Figure 4
House prices in Scotland, Wales and northern England have slipped further behind the national average since 1970. London and the south-east have forged further ahead, especially since 1980.

decline of the engineering industries and rising unemployment have clearly held down spending power and property values, in spite of the oil boom in the late 1970s. Average prices in Scotland fell from just on the national average in 1970 to 79 per cent of the average in 1987.

Regional house prices are in fact an excellent reflection of the health of the local economy. Prices in London and south-east England rose particularly fast during all three of the property booms in 1972–73, 1978–80 and 1986–88. During the two intervening recessions, in the mid-1970s and the early 1980s, the property market in London and the south-east was rather sluggish. In the recession of the mid-1970s, prices rose fastest in south-west England, and in both London and the south-east price rises were below the national average. During the recession in the early 1980s, house prices actually rose fastest in Scotland, bolstered by the prospering North Sea oil industries, and increases in London and the south-east again briefly ran below the average.

Regional averages do not tell the whole story. Within the various regions, prices in certain districts have risen much

Table 2
Regional house prices related to national average

Average UK house price, and regional prices as a proportion of it

	1970: UK £4,975	(%)	1976: UK £12,704	(%)	1987: UK £39,551	(%)
1	Greater London	138	Greater London	123	Greater London	161
2	South-east	125	South-east	122	South-east	140
3	Scotland	101	South-west	102	South-west	109
4	South-west	98	Scotland	102	East Anglia	102
5	East Anglia	91	Northern Ireland	101	West Midlands	82
6	West Midlands	90	East Anglia	93	East Midlands	80
7	Wales	89	West Midlands	92	Scotland	78
8	Northern Ireland	88	Wales	88	North-west	74
9	North-west	84	East Midlands	84	Wales	74
10	East Midlands	80	North-west	83	Northern Ireland	71
11	North	79	North	82	North	68
12	Yorks & Humb'side	73	Yorks & Humb'side	79	Yorks & Humb'side	68

1987 figures are for the 2nd quarter.
Source Building Societies Association

faster than prices in others. Spotting the up-and-coming properties can add to the fascination of buying a home.

The biggest increases have been in fashionable districts where money is no object. Central London alone, where property prices have been driven up by wealthy foreigners, diplomats and (most recently) successful bankers and share dealers, now contains several thousand homes that are worth at least a million pounds each. But the price of almost every house or flat in every part of the country has beaten inflation.

Why property prices rise

The reasons for the doubling of the real cost of property since 1960 have been the subject of lively and sometimes acrimonious debate involving the political parties, local authorities and council tenants – and first-time buyers struggling to save a deposit for homes which seem to stay mockingly out of reach.

Inflation, cheap and easy credit for home buyers, income tax relief on mortgage interest, the policies of building societies and other lenders, shortages of building land, and planning restrictions – all these factors have been blamed for pushing prices up and deepening the divisions between the 'haves' who are on the property ladder and the 'have nots' who are not.

But the behaviour of property prices is not only a social issue. Prices quite clearly rise faster than inflation at some times and more slowly at others. Trying to work out when property is 'cheap' (and prices are likely to rise faster than inflation) and when it is 'dear' (and price rises are likely to lag behind inflation) has become an extremely important subject for property buyers. Getting the timing right can get first-time buyers off to a flying start as home owners. Existing home owners wondering when to move up the ladder would also dearly love to know when to take on an extra borrowing commitment and when to wait.

Inflation has certainly helped to push up property prices, but property has risen twice as fast as inflation over the last 25 years, so inflation alone is not the only factor. What is more, the big rises in property prices in 1972–73 and again in 1978–80 took place *before* the peaks in inflation which came in

1974 and 1981 (see Figure 5). Time will tell whether the property boom of 1986–88 was the result of buyers' rushing into bricks and mortar in anticipation of another surge in general inflation.

But inflation alone is not the key to predicting property prices. Cheap credit has helped make buying property easier and has allowed more people to afford higher prices for a home. Mortgage loans are among the cheapest kinds of credit available – cheaper than bank overdrafts and personal loans, and roughly half the cost of getting credit on Access or Visa cards and most kinds of consumer credit.

During the 1970s, mortgage interest rates rose sharply, but there was no obvious link between mortgage rates and house prices. In 1972–73, mortgage rates began to look cheap compared with inflation, and house prices rose steeply, but in 1978–80 the second price surge coincided with record mortgage rates of 15 per cent. More recently, mortgage rates have come down again, but not as fast as inflation (see Figure 6). Mortgage rates have been more than double the rate of inflation, yet house prices have continued to rise. Changes in interest rates seem to have more effect than the absolute level of the rates.

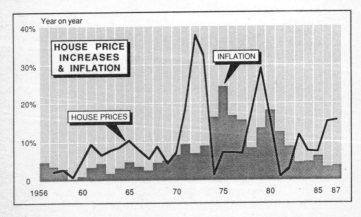

Figure 5
House prices jumped sharply in advance of inflation in the early and late 1970s. Prices have risen similarly in the 1980s. What happens now?

Income tax relief on mortgage interest makes mortgages even cheaper. The interest on the first £30,000 of a mortgage loan on a borrower's main home qualifies for income tax relief. If the basic rate of income tax is 25 per cent, the borrower effectively pays only 75 per cent of the interest which is due. Taxpayers who earn enough to pay tax at higher rates get an even better deal. Anyone who has to pay tax at 40 per cent pays only 60 per cent of the interest nominally due. Home owners are also exempt from all taxes on profits they make from selling their main home. Tax relief certainly makes a home an excellent investment, and it has significantly increased demand for property. But tax rates do not change often enough to explain why property prices accelerate and slow down again.

Mortgage availability

Inflation, cheap credit and tax advantages are all good reasons why housing has been seen as a good investment. But they do not explain why house prices periodically take off and then stagnate. In the 1970s, building societies often got the blame for fuelling house price rises by lending aggressively when they had plenty of money to lend and checking the market by rationing mortgages when they were not attracting enough

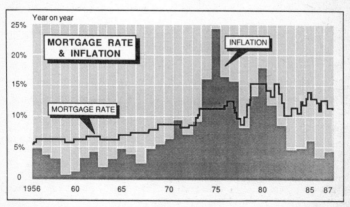

Figure 6
Mortage rates have tended to rise, but they were usually below inflation in the 1970s. After allowing for tax relief, mortgages were even cheaper.

savings to meet demand. It is certainly true that the flows of savings into the building societies do vary from month to month and year to year, and the amounts they lend also fluctuate in the same way.

Until recently, societies made the fluctuations greater by delaying changes in their interest rates when other interest rates – bank rates and the returns on National Savings – have changed. They maintained their rates partly because it costs them time and money to change rates and to notify all their customers. Successive governments also put pressure on societies when other interest rates were rising to draw on their reserves and keep mortgage rates down and the level of lending up, forcing societies to keep rates high and rebuild their reserves when other rates were coming down.

As a result, the supply of mortgage funds has fluctuated quite sharply from year to year. In 1975, for example, building societies lent almost 70 per cent more money than in 1974. But in 1979 and again in 1980 they lent only about 5 per cent more than in the previous year, with surprisingly little effect on house prices.

Societies also varied the proportion of property values which they would lend. When money was plentiful, societies would offer house buyers on average as much as 70 per cent of the value of the properties they were buying, but when funds were scarce the proportion could fall as low as 60 per cent, forcing some buyers to buy something cheaper, or preventing their buying anything at all unless they could arrange a top-up loan from an insurance company or bank. Inevitably, these shifts pushed up the price which some buyers could afford to pay at some times and artificially kept down demand for houses at other times. But once again, as Table 3 shows, the immediate impact on prices was less than might be expected, even when building societies had a virtual monopoly of the housing finance market.

In any case, lenders no longer have the ability to influence house prices by manipulating the cost or the availability of mortgage money. Competition has created a free market in money, and mortgage rationing is now a thing of the past. The arrival of competitors, first the banks and then the mortgage loan companies, has meant that building societies now have little choice but to change interest rates whenever necessary to maintain a plentiful flow of mortgage money, and so to meet the competition and protect their market share.

Building societies have also been forced to relax their lending rules and to advance to the average borrower both a higher multiple of his or her income and a higher proportion of the value of the property. Between 1980 and 1985, the average first-time loan went up from 75 per cent of the property value to 85 per cent, and existing home owners were able to push up the amount they could borrow from a mere 46 per cent of the property value in 1980 to 59 per cent in 1985 (according to the Building Societies Association).

The new lenders – banks and mortgage loan companies – are also more generous than the building societies were when they had a virtual monopoly. There seems little doubt that the ability to borrow more has had a once-and-for-all effect of increasing property prices in the last few years. But property prices have continued to fluctuate relative to the rate of general inflation.

Property supply and demand

There is a market for property, and supply and demand for it are not in constant balance. The supply of homes has been increasing steadily but rather slowly: the number of houses being built each year has fallen from a peak of over 400,000 in 1967 and 1968 to around 200,000 a year in the early 1980s. Most of the fall has been in council housing, but the number of new houses built in the private sector has also fallen, from over 200,000 a year to about 150,000.

The decline in house building has been balanced by a steep fall in the number of houses being demolished. In the 1960s, slum properties were being knocked down at a rate of nearly 100,000 a year. But as the worst housing has disappeared, and fashions have moved in favour of gentrification of old properties, slum clearances have dwindled to about 10,000 a year, and more older houses are being improved or converted into flats, adding about 20,000 units a year to the total housing stock.

As a result, the housing stock has risen gradually from 18.6

million in 1970 to 22.1 million in 1987, and it is still growing by just under one per cent a year, which is faster than the increase in population. In the private sector, at least, homes are in short supply only in areas where commuters have started to move in, especially in the green belt around London and other big cities, where planning has limited building.

Demand for housing is much more difficult to measure. The total population is now hardly growing at all, but the total number of separate households is still rising, as more old people go on living on their own, as families split up, and as young people leave home earlier than their parents did. Housing also now ranks very high on most people's list of priorities, partly because it has proved such a good investment over the last 25 years. The average home buyer is now willing to spend between 15 per cent and 30 per cent of his or her taxed income on buying a home.

Demand for property in the economic sense does not depend only on wanting some property. Wanting property is one thing, being able and willing to pay for it is another.

Table 3
Inflation, house prices and lending

Year	Inflation (%)	House prices av. (%)	House prices rise (%)	Lending growth (%)	Mortgage rate (%)	Loan/price ratio (%)
1975	25	11,945	8	69	11.1	63
1976	15	12,759	7	23	11.1	65
1977	13	13,712	8	13	11.1	65
1978	8	15,674	14	27	9.5	64
1979	17	20,143	29	4	11.9	59
1980	15	23,514	17	6	14.9	57
1981	12	24,503	4	13	14.0	62
1982	6	24,577	0	25	13.3	68
1983	5	27,192	11	27	11.0	68
1984	5	29,648	9	25	11.8	69
1985	6	31,876	8	8	13.5	69
1986	4	36,869	16	35	11.0	70

Table shows building society lending only. Figures are inflated in 1975 and 1976 when societies were gaining market share, deflated in 1981 and 1982 when banks invaded the market, and inflated again in 1983 and 1984 as societies fought back.
Sources Various

House prices and earnings

Borrowers' incomes and earning potential obviously must have a considerable influence on the prices they are willing to pay for property. Building societies, banks and other lenders reinforce the link by basing the amounts they will lend on a multiple of the borrower's annual income before tax, as well as on a proportion of the value of the property. Linking lending to incomes helps reinforce the link between incomes and property prices. The relationship is not fixed, however. Building societies used to limit mortgage loans to roughly 2.5 times the borrower's annual income. They also restricted loans to a maximum of 75–80 per cent of the value of older houses, rising to 90 per cent on a new house which had a ten-year builder's guarantee. First-time buyers were allowed to borrow rather more, but buyers who already owned a property were expected to reinvest the profits and borrow only what they really needed to finance a move up-market.

In recent years, competition between building societies, banks and other lenders has pushed the limits higher. Most lenders will now lend up to three times the borrower's main annual income, plus the amount of any other income, or anything from 2.25 to 2.75 times the combined income of a couple (although many lenders will restrict that to couples with professional qualifications and apply a lower age limit of 25).

Most lenders will also now lend up to 90 per cent of the value of a property (less on very expensive properties), and first-time buyers may be able to get 100 per cent mortgages provided the property is in good condition and at the cheaper end of the range. At the peak of the latest property boom, 100 per cent mortgages were relatively easy to get, and some lenders, mainly smaller building societies struggling to find a niche in the market, were willing to lend up to 4 times annual income to borrowers with professional qualifications and good prospects of promotion.

In the long run, demand for housing depends on buyers' being able and willing to pay the prices required. Many lenders insist that rising earnings are the key to property prices, and prices surge only when earnings (and especially real earnings after allowing for inflation) are rising strongly. But Figure 7 shows that house prices tend to accelerate prior to a jump in earnings, while Figure 8 shows that the three price surges in the last 15 years all sent house prices shooting up much faster than earnings were rising.

The factor missing from the equation is confidence. Prices have shot up in real terms at times when buyers have felt confident that the economic outlook is improving, unemployment is falling and the prospects are bright. If incomes are thought to be in danger of being squeezed by inflation or by taxation, or if the economy is slowing and unemployment is rising, young couples may decide to put off trying to buy a home and existing home owners may decide to sit tight instead of trying to move up the housing ladder. As a result, demand is likely to dry up and house prices are likely to stagnate.

The price/earnings ratio

The relationship between house prices and earnings is a very useful indicator to watch, however. Over the last 30 years, the ratio between average house prices and earnings has ranged from just under 3 in 1960 to 4.2 at the peak of the first house price boom in 1973 (see Figure 9). It fell back quickly to 3 again by 1977 because house prices failed to keep pace with

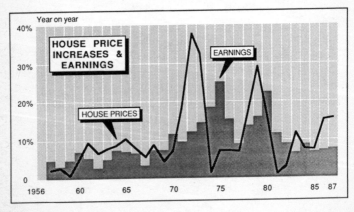

Figure 7
The peaks in house price increases in the 1970s anticipated rather than followed faster increases in earnings.

rapid increases in inflation and earnings. It went back up to 3.7 during the second property boom in 1979, slipped back to 3 again in 1982 and then climbed back to around 4 by the beginning of 1988. That figure included former council homes which had been bought below market value, and without them the ratio might have been considerably higher still.

The ratio of house prices to earnings also varies a great deal from one part of the country to another (see Figure 10). The index has traditionally been highest in London and south-east England, and lowest in northern England. In 1987, for example, although earnings in London and south-east England were higher than anywhere else in the country, home owners were paying 5.2 times their annual earnings for the privilege of living there, making it difficult if not impossible for first-time buyers without any capital to find even a flat which they could afford to buy. Even existing home owners were becoming very stretched to borrow the extra they needed to move up-market.

In northern England, Scotland, Wales and Northern Ireland, earnings were appreciably lower than in London but house prices were on average only 3 to 3.5 times average earnings. That made it easier for local people to buy property and get on to the housing ladder. But it had become difficult if

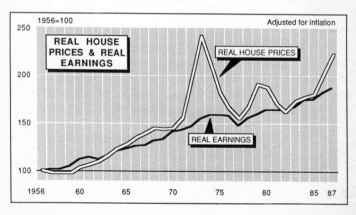

Figure 8
After allowing for inflation, prices and earnings have both risen over the years, but prices have surged ahead three times in recent years.

not impossible for northerners to move south or outsiders to move into London unless they had a large amount of capital, or had financial help from their family or employer.

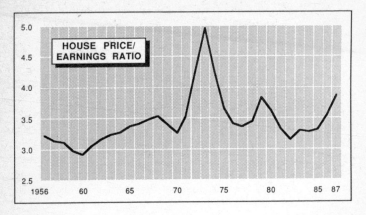

Figure 9
The ratio of average house price to average earnings has generally fluctuated between 3 and 4 — excluding the leap in the early 1970s.

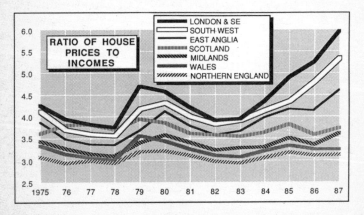

Figure 10
The ratio of house prices to earnings has generally been highest in London and the south, but recently the difference has become much more marked as prices in the south have raced ahead of earnings.

House prices in future

The combination of house prices averaging around 4 times earnings nationwide and 5 times earnings in the London area would normally mean that the boom in house prices was reaching its natural limits, and that further fast rises were either unlikely or potentially dangerous and unstable. Property prices in London and the south-east have also been linked to big salaries being paid in the City of London and to share prices on the stock exchange. A fall in share prices, and in the pay and commissions being earned in the City, is likely to affect local property values much more than in other parts of the country.

By the middle of 1987, the Bank of England had become nervous at the possibility of lenders making mortgage money too easy to borrow, and creating the risk of borrowers over-reaching themselves – perhaps getting into difficulties with repayments if interest rates rose or the economy began to slow down, incomes stopped rising and unemployment began to increase again. But the continuing fierce competition between different lenders means that mortgages remain much easier to get than in the past, and tax cuts and falling interest rates could help to offset any reduction in confidence on the part of home buyers.

The housing market in the UK as a whole is still developing. Home ownership is still rising slowly, and borrowers have not yet reached the limit of their ability to borrow. Many first-time buyers are close to the limits of what they can afford to borrow, especially in London and south-east England. But there is still scope for existing home owners to borrow more, and outside London the limits of prudent lending, measured by the house price/earnings ratio, have not yet been reached.

There are already signs that London-based firms are beginning to look outside London again to relocate or to expand, rather than pay the salaries needed to allow employees to buy the kind of homes they want in and around London. By the end of 1987, property values were actually rising faster in East Anglia and the Home Counties, and as far afield as Northamptonshire, than in London – and the ripple effect is expected to spread further out from the capital, encouraging faster increases in the east and west Midlands and in Yorkshire & Humberside in the next year or two.

2
The mortgage business

Housing finance is now big business. It is one of the fastest-growing and most successful sectors of the British economy. There are more than 240 different lenders – banks, building societies, insurance companies and mortgage companies – who between them have about £150 billion out on loan to help buy more than 6 million homes.

The role of the building societies is discussed in detail in Chapter 4. They have provided about three-quarters of all existing mortgage loans, although in mid-1987 their share of new mortgage lending fell to a record low – barely 50 per cent of the money lent and 60 per cent of the number of loans granted. The number of building societies has also been falling steadily, down to around 130 at the end of 1987, as a result of mergers and takeovers.

The societies' competitors are considered in Chapter 5. Most local authorities and other public sector lenders have been squeezed out of the mortgage market by government restrictions on public sector spending. But new commercial lenders have been encouraged to enter the business, including more than 50 banks, many insurance companies and a number of specialized mortgage companies, forcing the building societies themselves to become more commercial in their attitudes.

Competition between building societies and banks, insurance companies and mortgage companies for a share of what appears to be both a safe and a profitable business has drawn vast sums of money into housing finance and put unprecedented amounts of credit at the disposal of house buyers. The annual number of new mortgage loans has risen steadily over

the years from half a million a year in the 1960s to one million
a year in 1976 and 2 million for the first time in 1986. The
money lent each year has increased in even more spectacular
fashion, from £600 million in 1960 to over £2 billion in 1970,
£6 billion in 1975, £12 billion in 1980 and over £40 billion in
1987. Even after allowing for repayments, the net amount lent
each year has increased impressively, rising from £1.3 billion
in 1970 to £7.3 billion in 1980 and £30 billion in 1987.

Each year the building societies, banks, insurance companies and mortgage companies help about one-and-a-half
million people to buy homes, including about 750,000 first-
time buyers. Another 500,000 loans each year have been going
to existing borrowers who increased their mortgages mainly to
help finance home improvements. The 1988 budget removed
tax relief from home improvement loans. But the number of
loans will go on growing because the government has removed
the barriers to borrowers remortgaging their property to raise

Table 4
Market shares: new mortgages

Year	Net new loans (£m)	Share of new mortgage loans by lender (%)					
		Building societies	Local auth.	Insurance companies	Banks	Misc.	Other
1970	1,296	84	6	7	3	0	1
1971	1,878	85	6	4	5	0	1
1972	2,848	78	7	2	12	0	1
1973	2,893	69	12	6	11	0	2
1974	2,439	61	23	8	4	0	5
1975	3,730	74	17	4	2	0	4
1976	3,928	92	2	3	2	0	1
1977	4,362	94	0	3	3	0	0
1978	5,437	94	−1	1	5	0	0
1979	6,461	82	5	4	9	0	1
1980	7,333	78	6	4	8	0	4
1981	9,492	67	3	1	26	0	4
1982	14,137	58	4	0	36	0	2
1983	14,525	75	−2	1	24	2	0
1984	17,076	85	−1	1	12	3	0
1985	19,026	77	−2	1	22	2	0
1986	26,567	72	−2	1	20	9	0

more capital and building societies are allowed to make loans for any purpose.

Only 15 per cent of all house purchases each year are paid for in cash. The rest all depend partly on mortgage loans.

Mortgages

Mortgage loans secured by property are a very ancient form of borrowing, but the modern mortgage business has grown dramatically in the last few years. The number of borrowers doubled between 1980 and 1987 alone, and the volume of money lent more than tripled. In 1986 the value of mortgage loans on residential property in Britain overtook the value of all the existing loan stocks issued by the British government to finance its debts.

Residential mortgage loans are made specifically to help borrowers to finance the purchase of residential property. The loan is granted in return for a mortgage on the property, which

Table 5
Market shares: all mortgages

Year	Loans (£m)	Share of total mortgages outstanding (%)					
		Building societies	Local auth.	Insurance companies	Banks	Misc.	Other
1973	18,956	77	9	7	6	0	1
1974	21,373	75	11	7	6	0	1
1975	25,002	76	11	6	5	0	1
1976	28,856	78	10	5	5	0	2
1977	33,126	80	9	5	5	0	1
1978	38,533	82	8	4	5	0	1
1979	45,001	82	7	4	5	0	1
1980	52,424	81	7	4	6	0	2
1981	62,057	79	6	4	9	0	2
1982	76,214	75	6	3	14	0	2
1983	91,206	75	5	3	16	0	2
1984	108,564	76	4	2	16	1	1
1985	127,707	76	3	2	17	1	1
1986	153,666	76	2	2	17	2	1

Miscellaneous lenders include specialized mortgage companies.
Sources Financial Statistics Table 9.4; Building Societies Fact Book 1987

gives the lender the legal right to claim the property if the borrower fails to make the payments. Every month the borrower pays interest on the money borrowed. Instalments normally include *either* a repayment of some of the capital *or* a payment into an investment scheme which will provide a lump sum to pay off the mortgage when it matures – premiums on a with-profits or unit-linked insurance policy or contributions to a pension scheme. It is also now possible for middle-aged and elderly borrowers to take out an interest-only mortgage, where the loan itself is repaid only when the owner dies and the property is sold. The different types of mortgage are discussed in more detail in Chapter 6 and Chapter 7.

The borrower becomes the legal owner of the property bought with a mortgage loan as soon as the contract is signed, and is free to sell it at any time and redeem the mortgage. He or she also enjoys the profits if the price of houses rises, and suffers any losses if the price falls.

The borrower is also responsible for insuring the property and maintaining it in good repair. But the lender holds the deeds, which are the title to the property, as security for the mortgage loan. If the borrower fails to make the payments due within a reasonable period, the lender can foreclose the borrower, take possession of the property, and sell it to pay the outstanding debt.

The length of time a mortgage is to last is agreed in advance – normally 20 or 25 years, although it can be as little as 5 or 10 years or as much as 30 or 35 years, and in exceptional cases 40 years. But borrowers can redeem a mortgage early, and the average life of a mortgage loan has been getting shorter as selling up and moving becomes more and more common. Most people now move every five years or so, and even more often in London and the south-east.

Although the mortgage loan is a long-term one, lenders can normally change the interest charges borrowers have to pay, with little or no notice. This is necessary because lenders also have to adjust the interest rates they pay investors for deposits, in line with supply of and demand for savings and the general level of interest rates in the economy.

Building societies, in particular, still have to get over 80 per cent of the money they need from small investors' savings, much of it kept in accounts from which it can be withdrawn quickly if rates are no longer competitive – leaving building societies no choice but to keep pace with the market and to pass the changes on to borrowers. Conversely, if societies' interest rates are too high they can quickly be flooded with cash while borrowers will look for cheaper loans elsewhere. Lending rates and savings rates must then be brought down. Similar pressures apply to other lenders.

Only recently have some lenders begun to offer mortgage loans with the rate of interest fixed for longer periods – usually at least a year and sometimes as long as five years – by taking advantage of their ability to finance the loans out of money they themselves can now borrow at fixed interest rates in the London money market. But fixed-rate finance remains the exception rather than the rule.

Mortgage interest rates

The true cost of mortgages is slightly higher than the nominal rates of interest which lenders quote. Borrowers have to pay for the survey and legal fees and any 'arrangement' fees lenders may charge. Costs will also be affected by how often interest is added to the account and how often it is paid. Those costs affect all mortgages. In addition, borrowers who have repayment mortgages are paying slightly more because most lenders calculate the monthly payments due at the beginning of each year and make no allowance for any capital being paid off each month. The Consumer Credit Act requires all these costs to be taken into consideration in calculating the true cost of a mortgage. They can add roughly 0.5 per cent to the quoted cost of such a mortgage when interest rates are around 10 per cent, and as much as one per cent extra when nominal rates are around 15 per cent. (See Chapter 8.)

Interest rates have tended to rise over the last three decades. The rate charged by the building societies rose from roughly 4 per cent to 6 per cent during the 1950s, and from 6 per cent to 8 per cent during the 1960s. In the 1970s it ranged between 8 per cent and 15 per cent, and in the 1980s from 15 per cent down to 10 per cent. But throughout the period since World War II mortgage finance has been consistently cheaper than unsecured overdrafts and personal loans, and mortgage interest rates have sometimes been below the rate of inflation, with the result that borrowing yielded a profit instead of incurring a cost. With tax relief the true cost of mortgage money was lower still.

In the 1970s, mortgage rates rose significantly, but the rate of inflation rose higher still and for several years borrowers were not paying enough to compensate lenders for the fall in the value of money. In the 1980s mortgage rates have come down but not as fast as inflation, and borrowers have been paying interest rates which have been as much as 7 per cent above the annual rate of inflation.

Mortgages have also become slightly dearer in relation to interest rates in the rest of the economy as a result of the greatly increased competition for savings between banks, building societies and National Savings and other investments; the costs of this competition have been passed on to borrowers.

But increased competition means that there is no shortage of money to borrow, and the higher real cost has clearly not discouraged home buyers from borrowing. Even before tax relief, the interest rate on mortgages is usually between 1 and 2 per cent below the rate which banks charge private customers for overdrafts and personal loans. Mortgage loans are quite substantially cheaper than overdrafts because overdrafts and personal loans are unsecured but mortgage loans are secured by the value of the property itself, and the lender has the right to claim the property and sell it to repay the debt if the borrower defaults. With property prices rising almost every year since the 1950s, the risk of the lender losing money has been negligible.

Arrears and repossessions

The number of borrowers who get seriously in arrears with mortgage payments, and the number of properties repossessed because the borrowers have failed to make the payments, have been rising gradually in recent years. But the proportion is still relatively small. In 1985 building societies reported that about 0.91 per cent of all borrowers were more than six months behind with their payments, but only about 0.25 per cent, or one in every four hundred borrowers, fell so far into arrears that their homes had to be repossessed to repay the lender.

Building societies became a little tougher in 1986, pushing arrears down to 0.80 per cent and repossessions up to a record 0.3 per cent. Both figures rose slightly in 1987. But the figure is still far lower than the proportion of bad debts on personal loans and overdrafts.

Banks are less conscientious about collecting figures, and they claim fewer borrowers get into difficulties because banks rarely allow customers to borrow the full purchase price of the property. Borrowers who have paid for even 5 per cent or 10 per cent of their home have a bigger incentive to manage their affairs and stay out of financial difficulties compared with those with 100 per cent mortgages, who may feel they have nothing to lose.

But banks are not immune from defaults and arrears on their mortgage business. The Association of Metropolitan Authorities too has reported that borrowers with local authority mortgages have also been getting into arrears.

The problems of arrears and repossessions could however have been much worse, especially as house prices have spiralled and average mortgage payments have risen from £300 a year in 1970 to £3,000 a year in 1987. The problem has been kept under control partly because home owners are doubly reluctant to lose a sound investment as well as a home.

Anyone who qualifies for supplementary benefit is also entitled to have up to half their monthly mortgage interest payments paid by the Department of Health and Social Security for the first 16 weeks they are out of work. After that the DHSS will pay the mortgage interest in full, although it will not pay the capital payments or endowment premiums.

The sharp rise in unemployment is often blamed for the rise in the number of people in mortgage difficulties. But a study by the Bristol & West building society in 1987 showed that unemployment and illness account for only about 22 per cent of all cases where families get seriously behind with their

3
Tax relief – the billion-pound boost

The phenomenal rise in property prices in the last 30 years is at least partly due to the tax advantages governments have given to lenders and to borrowers. Building societies have been allowed to pay interest to investors after deducting a special low 'composite' rate of income tax, leaving basic-rate taxpayers with no further liability to tax. Building societies were also able to keep all profits from their investments in government stocks without paying tax, and as non-profit-making organizations they have largely escaped corporation tax.

In the last few years the government has tried to introduce a 'level playing-field', allowing banks as well as building societies to pay interest to savers after deducting the same 'composite' rate of income tax. Since 1983, building societies have also had to pay tax on their profits from trading in government stocks. But because they are mutual societies they are under no obligation to make profits to pay dividends, and the surpluses they make are still tiny – less than £1 per £100 of assets.

Home owners also continue to enjoy tax advantages which are not available on other investments. Profits made on the sale of the owner's own home are exempt from capital gains tax even if the owner makes other capital gains which exceed the annual tax-free allowance. If someone has two or more homes, only one home – referred to by the taxman as the owner's 'principal residence' – is exempt from capital gains tax but the owner can choose which house it is, provided he or she has lived in it at some stage.

Owner-occupiers are also allowed tax relief on the interest

charged on mortgage loans of up to £30,000. The income used to pay mortgage interest up to that limit is effectively free of income tax. If the full amount of interest is paid, allowance is made when your tax liability is calculated. But in many cases the tax relief is deducted from the interest bill before it is paid. Mortgage interest relief is allowed on only one home, but once again owners of more than one property can choose which house qualifies. Tax relief was originally given on all loan interest, but it has been restricted to interest on mortgage loans since 1969. Home improvement loans also qualified for tax relief until April 1988.

Tax relief reduces the interest borrowers have to pay, according to the rate of tax they are charged. A borrower paying 10 per cent on a £10,000 mortgage might expect to pay £1,000 a year in interest before tax relief. But if he or she pays tax at a basic rate of 25 per cent, or 25p in the pound, the actual interest paid is reduced to £750. The net rate can be calculated by doing a simple sum. Subtract the tax rate from 100; divide the result by 100; and multiply *that* result by the nominal interest rate. So if the nominal rate is 10 per cent and the tax rate 25 per cent the net rate actually paid is $10 \times (100 - 25)/100 = 7.5$ per cent. If the nominal rate is 9 per cent and the tax rate 25 per cent, the net rate is $9 \times (100 - 25)/100 = 6.75$ per cent.

The £30,000 limit

Tax relief made home ownership too good an investment for wealthy people who were heavily taxed on other investments, and in 1974 a ceiling was imposed on the amount of mortgage loan on which relief was given. But tax relief remains a unique advantage for home buyers – a subsidy which is not now available to individuals on any other kind of loan or credit. The limit was raised from £25,000 to £30,000 per person in 1983. Married couples get only a single allowance, but joint owners (including unmarried couples living together) who took out a joint mortgage before 1 August 1988 qualified for an allowance of up to £30,000 each, which they can use to get tax relief on a joint mortgage of up to £60,000.

The £30,000 limit refers to the amount borrowed, but the actual amount of tax relief is based on the amount of interest paid, and its value to the borrower also depends on the rate of income tax. If the limit remains unchanged the maximum amount of tax relief allowed increases when mortgage interest rates rise and falls when they come down. If the mortgage interest rate is 10 per cent, borrowers can get tax relief on interest payments of up to £3,000 a year. If the rate rises to 11 per cent, the allowance goes up to £3,300; but if the rate falls to 9 per cent, the allowance goes down to £2,700.

The amount of tax relief received on each pound of interest eligible for tax relief falls when income tax rates are reduced and rises if they are increased. If the limit is £30,000, the gross interest rate is 10 per cent and the basic rate of tax is 25 per cent, the maximum tax relief a basic rate taxpayer can have is 25p × 3,000 = £750.

MIRAS

Borrowers used to pay interest on their mortgages in full and claim tax relief by reducing the amount of income tax they paid. Employees were given extra tax-free allowances each year, based on the estimated amount of mortgage interest they would pay, and the amount of tax deducted from wages and salaries was reduced accordingly. The self-employed had to put in claims with their annual tax returns. Allowances changed every time tax or mortgage rates changed, and the system caused an increasing amount of work for the Inland Revenue.

The rules were changed in 1983 to introduce Mortgage Interest Relief At Source (MIRAS). Tax-free allowances for mortgage interest were dropped and the amount of tax taken from wages and salaries went up. But borrowers were allowed instead to deduct tax relief from the interest paid to the lender, and so reduce their monthly mortgage payments.

At first, only taxpayers with loans below the £30,000 limit for tax relief were included in MIRAS. But the system has gradually been extended, and since April 1987 almost all new mortgages have been brought into the MIRAS system.

For basic-rate taxpayers who have mortgage loans of £30,000 or less, the system is very straightforward. For every £1 of mortgage interest due each month, borrowers can reduce their interest payments by the standard rate of tax. Building societies, high-street banks and mortgage companies make this allowance automatically to all new borrowers, regardless of whether they pay tax and the rate of tax they pay. Self-employed people also benefit from tax relief at source instead of having to wait until they actually pay their taxes.

'Limited' loans

The system becomes a little more complicated for borrowers who have loans greater than £30,000, which used to be regarded as an exceptionally large amount but is now increasingly common as house prices continue to rise. In 1985, one in five of all new mortgages exceeded £30,000. In 1986 the proportion jumped to one in three, and in 1987 to nearly half. These are known in the mortgage business as 'limited' loans. Although tax relief is limited to the interest on loans up to the limit of £30,000 per person, borrowers with larger loans than that are also eligible for tax relief up to that amount. The result is two-tier interest rates – net rates with tax relief up to £30,000 and gross rates without tax relief above that level.

When MIRAS was first introduced, borrowers with limited loans were eligible to deduct tax relief from their payments only if the lenders were able and willing to allow it. Other borrowers with limited loans continued to pay interest in full and claimed the tax relief in the old way through an extra tax allowance, or by claiming for it in their annual tax return. Since April 1987, almost all lenders have brought new limited loans into the MIRAS system, but many borrowers with limited loans excluded from MIRAS before that date are still outside the system. 'Mixed' loans, where only part of the loan qualifies for tax relief, are also outside the system.

Higher-rate tax relief

The system is also more complicated for taxpayers liable to higher rates of tax. They are entitled to receive tax relief at source only at the standard rate of tax. Higher rate taxpayers can also claim extra tax relief, starting at their highest rate of tax, but the extra tax relief has to be claimed back in the old way through increased tax-free allowances and a consequent reduction in the amount of tax deducted from pay. A higher-rate taxpayer reduces his or her interest payments by 25p for every £1 of mortgage interest due, *and* claims another 15p in the pound back from the taxman, making home ownership a real bargain for the well-off.

The amount higher-rate taxpayers can claim back depends on their taxable income, which is calculated by deducting allowances from the amount actually earned. A married man living with or maintaining his wife in 1988–89 is entitled to earn £4,095 a year before paying tax. Income above that level is taxable, and the rate of tax increases as income exceeds certain levels. In 1988–89 he pays only the basic rate on the first £19,300 of taxable income. Above £19,300 a tax rate of 40 per cent applies.

So an income of £27,000 would leave him with a taxable income of £22,905, of which £19,300 would be taxed at 25p in the pound, and the last £3,605 at 40p. He would be entitled to deduct 25p in the pound from all the interest he pays on mortgage loans up to £30,000. He would also be entitled to a tax rebate of 15p in the pound on the first £3,605 of interest.

The system was even more complicated before the 1988 budget, when there were five different levels of higher-rate tax ranging from 40 per cent to 60 per cent.

Limited loans and higher-rate tax

Higher rates of relief only apply on amounts actually taxed at that level *and* only on the interest paid on mortgages up to £30,000. So if the gross interest rate is 10 per cent only the first £3,000 of interest is relieved of tax. If the gross interest rate is 13 per cent the first £3,900 is relieved of tax. The man in the example above would be able to claim higher-rate rebates on

£3,300 if the mortgage rate is 11 per cent. If the rate rose to 13 per cent and the gross interest to £3,900 a year, only the first £3,605 would be eligible for higher-rate relief because only that much of his income is subject to higher-rate tax; a further £295 would get basic-rate relief.

Tax subsidies

Tax relief, whether it is used to reduce the actual interest paid or it is reclaimed from the taxman, effectively scales down the true cost of paying mortgage interest. The system favours higher-rate taxpayers. If the mortgage rate is 11 per cent, anyone who earns enough to pay tax at the 40 per cent rate is really getting a slice of their mortgage for $11 \times (100 - 40)/100 = 6.6$ per cent. In 1987–88, someone paying tax at the top rate of 60p in the pound was actually getting some mortgage money at $11 \times (100 - 60)/100 = 4.4$ per cent interest.

The availability of tax relief has made home ownership an attractive investment as well as helping to satisfy a social need. Certainly it has encouraged home owners to buy more expensive homes than they would otherwise want to take on. Inevitably this has helped to push property prices higher than

Table 6
Net interest rates at various income tax rates

Gross interest rate (%)	Net interest rates (%) after tax relief	
	at 25% income tax	at 40% income tax
10.00	7.50	6.00
10.25	7.69	6.15
10.50	7.88	6.30
10.75	8.06	6.45
11.00	8.25	6.60
11.25	8.44	6.75
11.50	8.63	6.90
11.75	8.81	7.05
12.00	9.00	7.20
12.25	9.19	7.35
12.50	9.38	7.5

Figures valid for loans up to £30,000.

they might otherwise have gone.

Tax relief has also cost the Treasury more than £5 billion a year in lost income tax. The tax lost each year would be enough to pay for at least a 5p cut in the basic rate of income tax or to allow every taxpayer to earn an extra £1,000 a year before starting to pay tax.

Over the years, successive Chancellors of the Exchequer have tinkered with the system of tax relief. The limit on the amount of a mortgage which qualifies for tax relief was first imposed to try to discourage extremely wealthy individuals from investing too much of their assets in home ownership and starving their business investments.

The tax-free allowance has not been kept in line with the rise in property prices. It was first fixed at £15,000 and raised in steps to £25,000 in 1979 and £30,000 in 1983; since then it has remained unchanged. By 1987 it was not enough to cover fully a first-time buyer borrowing 90 per cent of the value of even an average home in London or in the more prosperous parts of the Home Counties. Tax relief was clearly not responsible for driving up property prices in many parts of the country to levels well in excess of the tax relief limit. It certainly did not contribute to the rise in property values that took place in the mid-1980s, and especially the very rapid rises in London in

Table 7

Effect of tax relief on net cost of mortgages

Amount of loan	Net interest paid by taxpayer			
	Basic-rate taxpayer		Top-rate taxpayer	
(£)	(£)	(%)	(£)	(%)
10,000	750	7.5	600	6.0
20,000	1,500	7.5	1,200	6.0
30,000	2,250	7.5	1,800	6.0
40,000	3,250	8.125	2,800	7.0
50,000	4,250	8.5	3,800	7.6
60,000	5,250	8.75	4,800	8.0
75,000	6,750	9.0	6,300	8.4

Table assumes a gross mortgage interest rate of 10 per cent;
a basic tax rate of 25p in the £; a top tax rate of 40p
(being paid by married man earning at least £23,395 in 1988–89).

1986 and 1987, which were financed by salaries and commissions earned in the City of London and the West End and by profits made on the stock market.

But, outside London and south-east England, tax relief is still a major incentive to take out a mortgage and buy a home. Tax relief is particularly valuable for the least well-off people and for first-time buyers, two groups of borrowers who tend to buy cheaper properties. It still fully covers the majority of loans taken out to buy homes outside London and the south-east. It is very useful for higher-rate taxpayers, who get tax relief at the highest rate of tax they pay. It also benefits unmarried couples who share homes and can claim tax relief on the interest on mortgages of up to £30,000 each taken out before 1 August 1988.

Tax relief is least valuable to buyers who do not earn enough money to reach the higher tax rates. It is also less useful to borrowers who can qualify for only one ration of mortgage tax relief, but still have to borrow more than £30,000 in order to buy the kind of home they need in the area where they intend to live.

The limit on tax relief allowed by the government was unexpectedly raised in 1983. Equally unexpectedly it was left unchanged in 1987. The value of tax relief has also been reduced by successive cuts in the basic rate of tax from 33 per cent to 30 per cent in 1979 to 29 per cent in 1984 to 27 per cent in 1987 and 25 per cent in 1988.

Future of mortgage tax relief

Tax relief is enormously popular with home owners and is now very difficult to abolish, because almost 10 million voters benefit directly or indirectly from it. But it remains a controversial issue. A number of tax reformers believe that tax relief on mortgages is inherently wrong, giving tax benefits to wealthy individuals who do not need them, helping to inflate property prices and diverting investment funds into housing and away from wealth-creating investment in British industry.

Mr Robin Leigh-Pemberton, the Governor of the Bank of England, when he was chairman of National Westminster bank and before the banks became active mortgage lenders, once condemned mortgage tax relief as a way of making Britons the best-housed poor in Europe.

The strongest critics of tax relief would like to see it abolished, either immediately or in stages, in order to release tax revenues which could be used (according to their political sympathies) either to finance other social policies or to cut the basic rate of income tax still further. Right-wing critics would also like to see tax relief abolished in order to make investment in homes less attractive and increase the incentive for individuals to put money into more productive investments.

Some critics want to see tax relief limited to the basic rate of tax, so that ordinary taxpayers receive no more and no less relief on each pound of interest than those who pay tax at higher rates. The introduction of MIRAS seemed to be a logical step towards confining tax relief to the basic rate of tax and giving every individual borrower the same amount of tax relief on every pound of interest paid. But the Chancellor was unable or unwilling to take the reform to its logical conclusion during the 1983–87 Conservative government.

Other experts would prefer to see the maximum amount of mortgage money eligible for tax relief firmly pegged at £30,000, so that inflation and increases in house prices over the years would gradually erode its value. As long ago as 1983 it was quietly taken for granted that the upper limit for tax relief would be pegged at £25,000 and the benefit would be allowed to wither rather than being abolished.

The limit was raised to £30,000 in 1983 only at the express wish of the Prime Minister, Mrs Thatcher, who believed increased tax relief to be politically and socially desirable. But since then it has remained pegged at the same level, despite the great leap in house prices during 1986–87.

Restricting tax relief to first-time buyers only is another option which is sometimes recommended. But it seems unlikely that any government would find it politically practical to restrict tax relief in this way. It would be highly unpopular with existing home owners who would lose their tax relief if they moved home and would force many of them to stay put in their first home, blocking the way up the housing ladder for new buyers.

It would also artificially increase the demand for rented accommodation which is already in short supply, because couples would try to save longer in order to buy a more expensive first home. It would penalize couples wanting or needing to buy a first home early in life when they could only afford a cheap property, and strip them of tax relief as soon as they moved on. There would also be problems in deciding whether divorced couples could requalify as first-time buyers or not.

The abolition in 1988 of four of the five higher rates of tax, leaving just one basic and one higher rate, has taken much of the heat out of the argument by reducing the amount of tax relief on mortgage interest along with the amount of tax paid on income.

Further tinkering is inevitable, whatever government is in power. But total abolition of mortgage tax relief does seem unlikely, even as part of a move to reduce the basic rate of income tax still further. Tax relief is a vital element in reducing the cost of repaying a mortgage. It is already of most value to first-time buyers, who tend to buy the cheapest properties available. Fewer first-time buyers would be able to afford to buy a home at current prices without the benefit of tax relief, especially in the less prosperous parts of the country.

4
Building societies – the old standby

The building societies were almost entirely responsible until recently for financing the expansion of home ownership which has taken place since World War II. Until the end of the 1970s they provided approximately 90 per cent of all mortgages.

Building societies are mutual societies. They have no shareholders, and are under no obligation to make profits or pay dividends, which allows them to operate on very narrow margins. Their operating costs average around one per cent of the money they handle, and their annual surpluses average just over one per cent before tax. But over 80 per cent of their funds come from small savers through the branch offices, which are in competition with banks and National Savings, which makes the average cost of raising money rather high.

Although the first building societies were formed over 200 years ago as housing clubs to build homes for members, their business grew only slowly until the 1950s. In 1950 there were over 800 societies with combined assets of about £12 billion. Less than half a dozen were truly national. About 200 were regional societies and the great majority were very local, concentrating on one or two towns, many of them operating through only a single office. Since then numbers have been reduced as a result of mergers, but the combined assets of the building societies have expanded very rapidly, overtaking the domestic banking system and National Savings, as well as the market in government stocks, in the process.

Building societies until very recently all paid the same basic rate of interest to investors, and charged identical mortgage rates recommended by the council of the Building Societies

Association. But they have always tried to compete in size, opening new offices to win new business. Big societies have taken over smaller ones, medium-sized societies have merged in order to climb up the league table and also to extend their office network and create more broadly based groups.

The Northampton Town & County society, for example, merged with the Leicestershire in 1966 to form the Anglia, which merged with the Hastings & Thanet in 1978. The enlarged Anglia then took over the London & South of England in 1983 and merged yet again with the Nationwide to form the Nationwide Anglia in 1987.

Many of the smallest societies have voluntarily looked for a larger partner in order to share the costs of refurbishing their offices and installing computers, and advertising and promo-

Table 8
Top twenty building societies, 1986

		Assets (£bn)	Borrowers (000s)	Average loan (£)	Branches
1	Halifax	28.69	1,491	16,100	729
2	Abbey National	23.04	1,109	17,400	676
3	Nationwide Anglia	17.57	863	16,800	930
4	Alliance & Leicester	8.10	417	16,200	421
5	Woolwich	7.83	363	17,900	412
6	Leeds Permanent	7.77	414	15,500	480
7	National Provincial	6.05	314	15,600	338
8	Bradford & Bingley	4.42	209	16,300	253
9	Britannia	4.21	214	16,300	245
10	Cheltenham & Gloucester	3.85	156	20,600	165
11	Bristol & West	2.54	106	18,500	168
12	Yorkshire	2.08	113	15,000	158
13	Birmingham & Midshires	1.86	103	14,700	143
14	Northern Rock	1.81	99	15,200	122
15	Gateway	1.76	85	17,000	150
16	Town & County	1.23	51	19,000	75
17	Coventry	0.97	53	14,500	61
18	Guardian	0.81	30	22,900	1
19	Skipton	0.80	45	14,100	57
20	Chelsea	0.76	27	22,300	51

Figures are for the end of 1986; the Nationwide and Anglia merged on 1 September 1987; the Woolwich and Gateway are merging in 1988.

ting their savings plans, and most recently recruiting specialists to manage their investments and advise on the best and cheapest ways of raising additional cash.

By 1980 the numbers had fallen to under 300 societies but their combined assets had risen to £53 billion. By 1987 numbers were down to under 150 and societies were disappearing at a rate of about a dozen a year. But assets by then had exceeded £140 billion.

Societies range in size from the giant Halifax, with assets of £30 billion and over 700 branches around the country, down to around 30 very local societies, each with assets of under £25 million and a single office. The five biggest societies now have over 60 per cent of the assets and are established in every part of the country. The top 20 societies have almost 90 per cent of the assets. But local societies still survive, thanks to local loyalties and local connections.

A number of societies both big and small – including the Cheltenham & Gloucester, the Guardian, the Regency, the Lambeth and the Peckham – look more favourably on larger loans as a way of holding down costs. Their average mortgage advance at the end of 1986 was in excess of £20,000, compared with a countrywide average of between £16,000 and £17,000.

Building societies' services

Rapid growth and concentration have been accompanied by a wider range of services and more profit-conscious policies. Until relatively recently, building societies were highly specialized and non-commercial organizations, subject to the rules of the Building Societies Act and governed by the Registrar of Friendly Societies. They were expected to make enough money to cover their costs but not to make profits, and they were certainly not expected to make a commercial rate of return on their assets. They accepted deposits almost exclusively from individual members of the public, who in turn could invest only a limited amount in any one society. Almost all societies paid the same rate, which they could change at seven days' notice.

Apart from their cash reserves, all the assets of societies had to be used to help finance house purchases, and until 1986 they had to direct 90 per cent of their loans to owner-occupiers. Within this 90 per cent individual loans were limited to a maximum of £20,000 until 1979, when the limit was raised to £25,000; it was later raised to £37,500 and then to £60,000 in 1982. A maximum of 10 per cent of their loans could be used to finance other forms of ownership, including the ownership of property for letting or shop accommodation, or invested in special mortgages in excess of the normal size limit, on which societies were allowed to charge higher interest rates. These limits were not abolished until the Building Societies Act of 1986 came into force.

In practice, only a handful of small societies, such as the City of London and the now defunct New Cross, took full advantage of that opportunity in order to create special niches for themselves and earn the extra interest needed to pay a fractionally higher rate on deposits. The majority of societies kept well within their guidelines. They were also required by the Registrar to keep at least 10 per cent of their assets in cash, or in investments such as gilt-edged stocks issued by the British government, which could quickly and easily be sold to provide cash to meet any sudden demands from investors to withdraw their money.

By comparison with banks and commercial companies, the building societies operated in a controlled and protected environment. Their skills were limited to assessing would-be borrowers, and the homes they wished to buy, in relation to the amount of cash the society had available.

Individuals wanting to borrow were judged by their income and circumstances and their ability to repay. The local branch manager decided the maximum amount he would be willing to lend to the individual. The society's surveyor then examined the property and decided its value, and the general management decided the percentage of current property values they would be willing to lend, depending on the supply and demand for mortgage money and how flush with funds the society was at the time.

If the would-be borrower qualified to borrow the amount he or she needed to buy the property, if the surveyor reported the value of the property justified a loan of that amount, and if the society had the money available immediately, the mortgage and the purchase could go ahead. If not, the society would turn down the application. The hopeful borrower would then have to try elsewhere, or look for a cheaper property.

In practice, societies were very conservative. When funds were in short supply, branch managers would be instructed to ration the money available to lend either by allotting mortgages each month on a first-come, first-served basis, or limiting them to existing customers who had saved money with the society for a certain period of time.

Societies were also very restrictive about the kind of people and properties eligible for mortgages. Until the 1970s, most societies were very reluctant to lend money to single women, or to take the earnings of a young married woman into consideration in deciding how much to lend, on the grounds that a woman might at any time become pregnant and have to stop work, with consequent loss of income.

They were also reluctant to lend money on flats, maisonettes or any converted properties, on the grounds that disputes could arise over responsibility for shared maintenance costs in blocks of flats or subdivided properties, or over the financial responsibility for damage to the borrower's property caused by neighbours. Any of these could make the property difficult to resell if the borrower failed to maintain the mortgage repayments. They were also often reluctant to lend on properties with sitting tenants, or on leasehold properties with less than 50 years of the lease unexpired, and also on older houses – especially large ones in which owners might let out rooms.

Societies were also ultra-cautious in their overall lending policies. They kept substantially more than the minimum percentage of assets required in reserves – usually nearer 20 per cent of their assets than the 10 per cent minimum required. The level of interest rates they could offer and the rates they could charge were decided by the Building Societies Association at its monthly meeting. The council and member societies preferred to change rates as infrequently as possible in order to minimize the administrative costs of calculating new monthly payments and sending out notices to all their customers.

Instead of varying interest rates, the societies drew first on their reserves to maintain the flow of new mortgages whenever they found difficulty in attracting sufficient savings to finance the current level of demand. If this proved inadequate to meet the demand for mortgages, societies would quickly resort to mortgage rationing by tightening their lending criteria or lending only to people who had previously been investors in the society. This continued until the flow of savings recovered or until an adjustment could be made to interest rates to rebalance the supply of savings with the demand for mortgage loans.

At times when the interest rates that societies paid on savings were high and the inflow of funds was heavy, societies relaxed their lending criteria, and made money more readily available for existing borrowers to borrow more for home improvements. Sometimes they quietly touted for new business by letting it be known they were flush with funds. But building societies were still under no pressure to make profits because they had no shareholders, and they took few risks. They were able to take advantage of a near monopoly of the mortgage lending business and they tended to be old-fashioned and paternalistic.

In the last decade their world has been progressively changed by the abolition of the interest-rate cartel, the entry of many new competitors into the mortgage market and the introduction of new freedom to invest and make commercial decisions. Some traces of their traditional attitudes may still remain in local branches, but the bigger societies have become increasingly sophisticated and competitive, and offer a growing range of savings schemes and financial services to support their traditional business. The bigger societies began offering cheque books and cash dispensers.

The interest-rate cartel began to break down during the 1970s, when a number of societies decided to offer higher rates of interest on certain types of savings accounts especially to attract larger sums of money or to retain it for longer periods. The rates paid on these accounts were based on the seven-day-notice rate, but investors were guaranteed a premium, usually 1–2 per cent above the ordinary rate. The new accounts proved very attractive to investors, and the proportion of savers' funds in premium accounts rapidly overtook the traditional share accounts.

The seven-day-notice account has remained the base to which premium account rates have been linked. But in 1982, under pressure from government competition policy, the Building Societies Association became only an advisory body doing no more than recommending rates. By 1985 even that role had been abandoned and societies were freed to decide their own savings and mortgage rates and the timing of any changes, without even a guideline from the Association.

Building societies today

Building societies now operate under the rules laid down by the Building Societies Act of 1986, which came into effect on 1 January 1987. It was a radical reform designed to make societies much more competitive and to encourage them to diversify gradually into other areas of activity. But it is already recognized that it will seem restrictive within a few years, and further reforms will be needed to keep pace with change.

The Act allows societies to provide many more services and to dabble in banking and broking as well as deciding whether or not to lend individuals the money they need to buy a particular house. To finance their increased range of services they are now allowed to borrow up to 40 per cent of the money they need from the London money markets instead of the traditional (and nowadays more expensive) method of attracting savings from small investors.

Societies with assets of over £100 million are also allowed to use up to 5 per cent of their total assets to provide personal loans for purposes other than housing; and large societies can buy land and build houses for sale. All societies can act as brokers, selling insurance policies, unit trusts, pension schemes, shares and personal equity plans – either as independents, offering a choice of products, or as representatives, selling the products of just one insurance company. They can own and operate subsidiaries including estate agents, selling houses as well as financing their purchase.

Differences between individual building societies, and especially between the big societies and small societies, are becoming increasingly sharp. The major societies called special meetings to obtain permission to extend their activities and the dozen or so biggest societies all started making personal loans and offering broking services soon after the new Building Societies Act became law on 1 January 1987. Some societies, led by the Halifax, the Abbey National and the Nationwide Anglia, have already begun building up chains of estate agents, and others are likely to follow. Some have developed special mortgage schemes such as the shared equity loans offered by the Nationwide Anglia and the Woolwich (see Chapter 12) or special packages such as the Cheltenham & Gloucester's Gold Loan, which offers cheaper mortgages to applicants who want to borrow at least £50,000 so long as it is not more than 75 per cent of the value of the property.

The smallest societies, with assets of less than £100 million, are not allowed to offer unsecured loans or become property developers. Most of them still offer only the traditional service, and competition is already further reducing their role. Many of them are too small to adopt complicated modern computer systems to monitor and control an increased range of services, and lack the specialized financial skills to market such services effectively. The number of societies is expected to go on falling to under 100. But most of the survivors will have a strong local base or a specialized appeal, which will ensure a valuable element of choice and variety for borrowers.

Some of the small societies, including the Peckham, the Stroud & Swindon, the West Bromwich and the Universal, have carved a niche by offering lower interest rates for first-time buyers; the Cumberland and the Coventry have offered 100 per cent loans to customers who have saved with the society; the Ilkeston and the Coventry have offered 100 per cent loans to council tenants wanting to buy their homes. The Manchester offers attractive rates to customers who want to borrow no more than 60 per cent of the value of the property, and the Mornington is willing to lend on accommodation which goes with shops, and property with sitting tenants. The Norwich & Peterborough has been one of a few building societies willing to offer bigger mortgages and deferred interest schemes to borrowers with professional qualifications and good prospects for the future.

Most of the larger societies have decided to remain independent agents, and offer borrowers a choice of different insurance companies' endowment policies and investment-linked and pension mortgage schemes. But the Abbey National has signed a deal with Friends' Provident to act as an agent, selling only the one company's insurance policies and packaging those policies with the society's loans. A growing number of smaller societies are also choosing to sign up as 'representatives' acting as tied agents for one or other of the large insurance companies. The Chelsea and Swansea building societies, for example, have signed a deal to sell only Guardian Royal Exchange products, the Staffordshire has signed up with Scottish Life, Universal with Commercial Union, the West of England and the Eastbourne Mutual with Legal & General, the Tipton & Coseley with Sun Alliance and the Portman with Scottish Life.

It is a moot point whether societies as a whole were pushed into providing a wider range of activities by a Conservative government determined to break up the traditional boundaries of banking and finance in Britain, or whether they welcomed the opportunity to flex their muscles, learn and develop new skills and compete.

Certainly there are some old-fashioned building society managers and staff who worry that building societies will lose their distinct identity – and the undoubted trust of both investors and borrowers alike – if they are drawn into more commercial activities which require aggressive marketing and tougher methods of credit control. Most older customers were initially opposed to change, according to a Gallup Poll in 1986. But the building societies were left with little option when outsiders began to invade their traditional territory and offer mortgage loans in direct competition with the societies themselves. Societies' share of the market in new mortgages fell from 89 per cent in 1980, the year the clearing banks began seriously competing in the mortgage market, to 77 per cent in 1983, before recovering to 80 per cent in 1986.

They recovered by increasing the choice of mortgages they

offered, by streamlining their methods of assessing borrowers and properties, and by taking a more generous view of the amount they would be willing to lend to borrowers, especially on older houses and flats. In the 1970s, borrowers had a choice of only two different types of mortgage: repayment and endowment-linked. By the mid-1980s, all the leading building societies had three or four different types of repayment mortgage, four or five different endowment mortgages and a range of pension-linked mortgages on offer. For details see Chapters 6 and 7.

In the 1970s, building societies were reluctant to lend more than 2.5 times a borrower's annual income or to take second incomes into consideration. In the last few years, the multiples have been creeping higher. At the height of the housing boom in 1987, only a few societies set limits as low as 2.5 or 2.75 times income. Most published a limit of 3 times first income, a few offered to go as high as 3.25 or 3.5 times, and it was possible to find societies willing to lend up to 4 times first income in exceptional cases. Not all borrowers pushed their limits, and the average loan was well below the maximum, but the average building society loan has been creeping up in relation to borrowers' average incomes. The *average* advance to first-time borrowers was only about 1.8 times annual income up to 1982, but it had edged up to 2.0 times income by 1986. The *average* advance to existing owner-occupiers has also increased – about 1.7 times annual income up to 1982, rising to 1.9 times income in the mid-1980s.

Down-market lending

The trend to financing the purchase of older properties began before these recent radical changes. Almost 30 per cent of the homes in Britain were built before 1919, but in 1970 only 17 per cent of building society mortgages were given to finance the purchase of these older properties, compared with 27 per cent advanced to help buy new homes. In the second half of the 1970s, older homes took around 23 per cent of new building society mortgages and loans on new homes dropped below 20 per cent – partly because of the drop in house building. Since

1980, well over a quarter of new mortgages each year have gone to finance the purchase of older homes, and new homes have accounted for little more than 10 per cent.

Building societies have also relaxed their traditional prejudice against flats and maisonettes. These accounted for only 4 per cent of building society mortgages in 1970, 9 per cent a decade later and consistently over 10 per cent in the 1980s. Mortgages on terraced homes rose from 20 per cent of all mortgages in 1970 to 30 per cent in 1980 and 34 per cent by 1986, while the shares of semi-detached houses, detached houses and especially bungalows all shrank.

Societies also became more liberal in advancing a bigger proportion of the value of properties. Advances to existing home owners averaged about 55 per cent of the price in the 1970s, and fell below 50 per cent in 1979 and 1980. But by the mid-1980s they were running at around 60 per cent.

First-time buyers also benefited; their average advance rose from about 75 per cent of the house price in the 1970s to 85 per cent from 1982 onwards. In the 1970s, less than 2 per cent of first-time buyers were able to borrow the full purchase price of their homes. In 1986, 32 per cent of first-timers were able to get a 100 per cent mortgage – though the percentage fell back again in 1987.

Societies have also played a significant part in helping council house tenants to buy their own homes. In 1982 and 1983, for example, over 15 per cent of building society mortgage loans went to council house tenants, most of them to buy the homes where they were living. Nationwide Anglia now operates a shared equity scheme for employees of the National Health Service, lending them money at cheap rates of interest in return for part of the profit if they sell the property (see Chapter 12).

Many building societies have also taken an active part in helping to finance urban renewal, lending to housing associations and to groups of craftsmen building their own homes. They also lend to help finance sheltered housing for elderly people and shared-ownership schemes, where individuals buy only part of a home initially, with the option to buy the rest at a later date (see Chapter 12). Building societies also actively moved into the market for further loans to help existing borrowers finance central heating, double glazing, re-roofing and other home improvements, which also helped them protect their share of the total mortgage market (see Chapter 10).

Building societies have increased their assets by between 14 per cent and 21 per cent a year since 1970, an average growth of 17 per cent a year in cash terms and 6 per cent a year above the rate of inflation. From a low point in 1982 of under 60 per cent of the money going into the new mortgage market, building societies rebuilt their share of the market to 85 per cent in 1984, and the banks' share fell back from 36 per cent in 1982 to 12 per cent in 1984.

Competition remains severe, however, and the societies' share of the market in new mortgages came under heavy pressure again from 1985 onwards as a determined attack on the mortgage market was launched, first by the clearing banks, then the foreign banks and the new mortgage companies working with insurance companies and through brokers and estate agents. By the middle of 1987, building societies were lending only about 50 per cent of the money going into new loans, compared with 30 per cent from the banking sector and 20 per cent from the mortgage companies.

The societies retained a rather larger share of the total number of new mortgages, but the quality of their new loan business had worsened, as banks and mortgage companies picked up more of the bigger loans to wealthier borrowers, leaving building societies with higher proportions of smaller loans which are more costly to administer, and of high valuation loans where there is a greater risk of loss to the lender if the borrower fails to repay.

Building societies in future

Building societies still have considerable natural advantages. They are still under no obligation to make profits and their administrative costs are still relatively low. But they have been operating under the handicap of relying heavily on deposits from small savers. Building societies have to offer relatively high rates of interest to compete with National Savings, and their average borrowing costs are higher than the costs which banks and mortgage companies have to pay in the London money market. Societies have already been forced to ask permission to borrow more heavily in the money market, and they are under increasing pressure to review their traditional role as a form of social service. Competition has obliged them to consider imposing higher interest rates on smaller loans – the exact reverse of the situation prior to 1980. The Abbey National has already announced plans to convert itself into a public company and raise capital by selling shares to investors, functioning like a bank rather than a building society. Other societies will probably follow its lead.

5
The competition –
new lenders

Local authorities were at one time the building societies' biggest competitors. In the 1960s a number of local authorities began offering mortgage loans, and by 1970 they accounted for almost 10 per cent of the new loans granted each year. Most of the money for mortgage lending came out of long-term capital and they did not have to adjust interest rates as quickly as the building societies. But they were in competition with building societies only to a limited extent.

In particular, local authorities lent to people living in the inner city areas, where the great majority of houses were built before 1919, property was often in a dilapidated condition as a result of years of neglect, and borrowers found building society mortgages difficult to get. Building societies were equally reluctant at the time to offer mortgages on either flats or maisonettes.

Building societies which were willing to offer mortgages on such properties were usually willing to lend only 50 per cent of the asking price or less, and few families in inner city areas had anything like the savings required to pay the balance of the purchase price. Neither did they have the money to make the immediate repairs and improvements most building societies would think necessary to justify a decision to lend.

Local authorities had built up a substantial stock of council homes. But even Labour-run councils wanted to encourage more private tenants to buy and become owner-occupiers, and to improve run-down properties to increase their rateable value. Also, they were able to borrow long-term capital at the lowest available interest rates, including loans for up to 30 years at fixed rates of interest from the government-run Public Works Loans Board.

Many authorities, including the Greater London Council, set aside substantial amounts of capital to fund mortgages, and adopted easier and more flexible lending conditions than building societies, including fixed-rate mortgages. Many authorities would lend a higher multiple of the borrower's income than the societies, and a higher proportion of the value of the property.

Some authorities were willing to lend as much as 100 per cent of the value of the property, to spread repayments over periods of 30 years or more, and to offer low initial repayments. The government also helped local authorities to offer low-cost mortgages, some building societies lent surplus money to local authorities for their mortgage programmes, and for a few years local authorities were a significant force in the mortgage market. In 1974, when they were lending cheap money and building societies were rationing mortgages, local authorities briefly accounted for almost a quarter of all new mortgage loans.

But demand was so great that most authorities began to run out of capital, and the rate of repayments was not enough to sustain the level of lending required. The building societies responded to competition by relaxing their rules on providing mortgages on older properties and flats, as well as financing sales of council housing.

The political climate also changed. Some Labour-controlled local authorities took fright at the prospect of helping to create a majority of owner-occupiers, who might be expected to vote Conservative. All local authorities, including Conservative-controlled ones, came under pressure to reduce their capital spending, and mortgage lending programmes were an early casualty of local authority spending cuts. Local authorities' share of the market fell from 9 per cent of all new mortgages in 1970 to 7 per cent in 1980, and since 1983 mortgage repayments to local authorities have been running ahead of new lending. Some authorities began selling mortgages to other institutions in order to get the capital back faster.

The banks

In the 1960s and 1970s the big London-based clearing banks and the Scottish banks did relatively little mortgage lending, although they had always offered housing loans at subsidized rates of interest to their own employees. The banks criticized the tax relief given for house purchase and the tax privileges enjoyed by building societies, which allowed societies to deduct a special low rate of tax on the interest paid to savers and to pay virtually no corporation tax.

During the house price boom in the early 1970s, a number of secondary banks and finance houses were attracted by the prospect of making safe loans at high rates of interest to home owners. Some began offering second and even third mortgages on homes whose value had risen well above the amount of the first mortgage, and borrowers were thus able to raise extra capital. New borrowers were also able to get top-up mortgages to put alongside building society mortgages and so were able to buy properties at prices which their own savings and a single mortgage would not have allowed.

But the share of the total mortgage market held by secondary banks was never significant, and the sharp rise in mortgage rates in the mid-1970s and a setback in property prices caused problems for many borrowers who had turned to second mortgages. Dozens of secondary banks and finance houses also got into difficulties, and the second mortgage market very quickly dried up. Recently some finance houses have returned to the mortgage market, setting aside capital for mortgage brokers to package into mortgages. UDT, the finance house subsidiary of the Trustee Savings Bank (TSB), offers its own service, Mortgage Express. But the total share of the business held by finance houses is still insignificant.

High-street banks

The high-street banks moved into the mortgage market during the 'Barber boom' in the early 1970s, but quickly cut back again when the government tightened lending controls. With the return of a new Conservative government in 1979, however, the banks themselves came under increasing pressure to compete and be more commercial in their attitudes, and they decided to take advantage of the easing of government guidelines on lending and hit back at the building societies by moving into the mortgage lending market. The TSB started offering mortgage loans in 1979 and the big clearing banks moved into the market in 1980.

Initially they concentrated on providing larger mortgages, an area to which the building societies had traditionally given a low priority, where the banks could take advantage of unsatisfied demand and charge a slightly higher rate of interest. Administrative costs were also proportionately lower on large mortgages, and banks could make a commercial profit on this business without challenging the building societies head on.

But the banks quickly began to move down-market. By 1982 the big four clearing banks – National Westminster, Barclays, Lloyds and Midland – plus the TSB and the Scottish banks were responsible for over a third of all new mortgages. Although the banks rapidly built up the market share they were looking for, and in 1983 halved the number of new mortgage loans they made, by the mid-1980s there were one million bank mortgages in existence, and the banks were still providing 15–20 per cent of all new mortgage loans.

The banks publish fewer figures than the building societies, but it seems certain that the banks have tended to stay slightly up-market. The average mortgage loan from a bank is rather larger than the average from a building society, and banks are reluctant to advance more than 90–95 per cent of the value of a property. Most of their customers already have a bank account and probably no more than one in four borrowers from the banks is a first-time buyer, compared with almost half the borrowers from the building societies. But there is a significant overlap of business, and the banks have created genuine competition in the mortgage market.

Right from the beginning, the banks set their mortgage interest rates without any reference to the building societies. They were able to take advantage of the fact that mortgage loans made up only a small part of their lending business as a whole, and small-scale savings only a modest part of the money the banks themselves use to finance that lending. The clearing banks, with the exception of National Westminster and the TSB, also calculate their lending charges slightly differently, reducing the capital outstanding (on which interest is calculated) monthly or quarterly instead of just once at the beginning of each year, so that the same nominal interest rate as a building society mortgage will result in a slightly lower annual interest charge. But banks may charge commitment fees. These have to be included in calculating the annual percentage rate of interest, which is the fairest method of comparing the true cost of mortgages. (See Chapter 8 for details.)

Competition triggered a number of changes in the mortgage market. A number of existing borrowers were tempted to pay off their existing mortgages and remortgage their properties with a bank. The building societies in turn responded, and stole business away from banks. Another consequence of increased competition was the disappearance of the premium interest rates charged on larger mortgages and on insurance-linked 'endowment' mortgages. Mortgage rationing became a thing of the past. A mortgage loan became a commercial service freely available to everyone with the right credit rating rather than a scarce commodity which individuals would have to qualify for.

Merchant banks, led by Hambros and Kleinwort Benson, have also moved into the mortgage market, acting either as intermediaries or as lenders in their own right. Foreign banks with branches in Britain also saw an opportunity to build up their sterling lending business in a relatively risk-free sector. They began by offering mortgages mainly if not exclusively to their own citizens posted to work in Britain and to employees of companies based in their home countries.

Once established, these banks quickly began to advertise and offer individual mortgages to other borrowers, often at interest rates linked to the cost of money in the London money market, where they raise most if not all of their finance. They still tend to specialize in larger-than-average mortgages for businessmen, and still concentrate heavily on property in London and the home counties.

Foreign banks are relatively cautious in the percentage of the property's value they like to lend, especially as they lack the traditional skills of a building society in vetting applications. In practice, relatively few first-time buyers will qualify for loans. But their interest rates and the times at which rates are raised or lowered often differ from those of building societies and British banks, and they do add still further to the competition and available choice. The American banks have been especially active. Citibank, in particular, has introduced some specialized types of mortgage, including 'Cap & Collar' mortgages, which offer borrowers greater stability by setting maximum and minimum interest rates. They offer fixed-rate mortgages when conditions are favourable, and also mortgages at rates linked to the London money market. The first Cap & Collar mortgages guaranteed rates no lower than 8.5 per cent and no higher than 11 per cent for the first five years.

But the American banks are not alone in the market. The Canadians are represented through Canada Permanent and Western Trust & Savings. The Dutch-owned ABN, the Bank of Kuwait and Bank of Ireland are active lenders. The Japanese banks, especially Sumitomo, have also been building up the expertise needed to move into the mortgage market in a big way, recruiting experienced local staff from both banks and building societies.

Mortgage companies

More recently still, a number of specialized mortgage companies have been set up to compete in the housing finance market, borrowing their funds entirely from big commercial investors or from the London money markets. The National Home Loans Corporation (NHLC) was set up in 1985 by a group of investors including banks and pension funds, and its own shares are listed on the stock market for ordinary investors to buy. The Household Mortgage Corporation (HMC) was formed in March 1986 by a group of banks, insurance companies and investment management companies. The Mortgage Corporation (TMC), another specialist mortgage company, is owned by Salomon Brothers, the American investment bank.

Mortgage companies borrow most of the money they need to finance their mortgage lending at wholesale rates of interest in the London money market or the international currency market, and make no attempt to attract savings from the small private investor. They offer mortgages in direct competition with the banks and building societies. But they set their mortgage interest rates quite independently, and they have tended to concentrate on the top end of the market, lending larger amounts but lower proportions of the property value and attracting the richer borrowers, especially existing home owners living in the London area.

The NHLC started off taking over mortgage loans from local authorities and other institutions who wanted to sell their loan portfolios. But it quickly moved into the business of marketing its loans through a number of intermediaries, including mortgage brokers and estate agents, and some leading insurance companies, who supply the endowment policies and pension plans to go with them. The NHLC also markets mortgage packages for other lenders including Barclays bank, helping the bank reach the customers of other banks, who would not approach Barclays directly.

The NHLC offers a maximum of 75 per cent of the value of a property, rising to 95 per cent if the borrower takes out a mortgage indemnity insurance policy, which will pay the extra if the borrower gets into financial difficulties and fails to maintain payments. Its conditions rule out practically all first-time buyers. Borrowers are offered a choice of a conventional mortgage interest rate, or of paying 1 per cent over the rate the banks themselves pay in the London money market (LIBOR – London Inter Bank Offered Rate). This has tended to be anything from 0.5–1 per cent below the rates charged by banks and building societies, and within two years of the NHLC's starting in business over half the company's customers were choosing to pay the rate linked to the money market interest rate.

By then, more than 40 per cent of the loans being granted were remortgages as existing home owners took out new loans, often at lower rates of interest. Many of these new loans were for larger amounts, so that home owners could pay off their original mortgages and leave themselves with some capital to spend in other ways.

The HMC also raises the money it needs on the London money market and channels the bulk of its mortgages through a panel of 10 leading insurance companies which have more than 400 branches between them. TMC raises the bulk of its money by issuing securities backed by the mortgages it holds. It is the only one of the three specialized mortgage companies that advertises mortgages in the press and financial magazines, inviting individual borrowers to apply by post or phone direct to the company – although it also offers loans through brokers and other financial intermediaries.

Securitization

The mortgage companies have added a new element to the market. They have also taken the lead in creating a secondary market in mortgages in Britain, allowing them to treat mortgage loans as securities which they can pass on to other investors so as to refinance their own activities and build up funds to expand their lending business without waiting for the slow process of repayments to build up.

The idea of 'securitizing' mortgage loans began in the United States, and was approved in Britain only after much debate and the establishment of rules to protect borrowers from any possible exploitation and harassment. Lenders may now sell mortgages off in bulk to other institutions, usually banks and pensions funds, or use them as security to raise money from investors who are looking for a secure investment with a high rate of interest but do not have the expertise to offer mortgage loans on their own account.

Borrowers must give their consent to having their mortgages transferred to a different investor, and the original lenders must continue to administer the mortgages they have issued. They are also obliged to keep the rate of interest charged in line with what they charge new borrowers, so that borrowers whose mortgages are sold cannot be treated differently.

In the past, only a limited number of financial institutions – building societies, banks and insurance companies in particular – have had the resources needed to lend money which could be tied up for as long as 30 or 40 years. That situation is now changing fast. By securitizing mortgages, a growing number of financial services groups and traditional lenders, who have expertise in assessing mortgage proposals and access to potential borrowers, can arrange mortgage loans and recycle them to make more mortgage loans without tying up vast amounts of capital. They also earn a fee for continuing to manage the original mortgage and collecting the payments due.

Insurance companies

Until recently, insurance companies have played an important but almost entirely passive role in the mortgage market. The Prudential offered mortgages in the 1960s but subsequently dropped out of the market. Most insurance companies, like the banks, confined themselves to giving mortgages to employees.

At times, insurance companies have also offered top-up mortgages to borrowers unable to borrow enough from a building society to purchase the home they want. Top-up loans were particularly important in the 1970s, when building societies were unable or unwilling to increase the size of their biggest loans to keep pace with rising property prices. Borrowers who found they could not borrow as much as they needed had to turn to insurance companies for the extra money, often at a higher rate of interest, and take out an endowment policy which would repay it.

Top-up loans helped to give insurance companies and pension funds a 10 per cent share of the mortgage market in 1970. As building societies became more commercial, however, the insurance companies' direct lending role began to diminish, their share of the market for new mortgages falling to only 2 per cent in the first half of the 1980s. In the hectic housing market of the mid-1980s, top-up mortgages were again in demand by borrowers needing more than the average building society or bank would lend, but in the mortgage market as a whole top-ups are still unimportant.

But insurance companies play a vital role in the housing

finance market by providing the endowment insurance policies to go with endowment mortgages offered by other lenders. With these mortgages, borrowers pay interest on their loans but do not make direct repayment of any capital. Instead, they pay premiums on endowment insurance policies; the premiums are invested by the insurance company to build up capital to repay the mortgage in a lump sum, and usually provide a tax-free bonus as well.

Insurance companies have always been active in devising new products. Norwich Union and Royal Life were amongst those who introduced the first cheap endowment policies in the 1960s, and Abbey Life the first mortgage backed by unit-linked investments in 1982 (see Chapter 6). Insurance salesmen also made informal contacts with mortgage brokers and estate agents and paid commission on the insurance business which was introduced to them.

Endowment mortgages were until recently less common than repayment mortgages. Lenders charged higher interest rates on them, and insurance companies had little chance of advertising them. The change in tax rules associated with MIRAS (see Chapter 3) and the growing popularity of endowment mortgages greatly increased the demand for endowment policies, however, and insurance companies began actively to market their own endowment insurance policies to borrowers instead of waiting passively for business. Foreign banks and mortgage companies with few outlets of their own also began to link up with insurance companies to market mortgages through their branches.

A small number of insurance companies have started using their own funds to provide mortgage loans as well as endowment policies. Allied Dunbar, one of the newer generation of insurers, has always advertised and sold its insurance policies direct to the public. More recently it has begun to market mortgages in the same way, using its own money. The Co-operative Insurance Society also markets mortgages using its own money.

The Prudential and the Pearl, both of which have large direct sales forces who call on individuals at home, have acted as unofficial agents for mortgages for years. Both groups have now organized their branches and begun actively marketing mortgage packages using their own policies. But the actual mortgage money still comes from other lenders – and the Pru and the Pearl have not been lending their own funds.

Other insurance companies such as Norwich Union have no direct salesmen, and market their policies through independent brokers and financial intermediaries, who can offer individual borrowers a choice of lender. They have also been leaders in a campaign to help independent insurance and mortgage brokers to comply with the requirements of the new investor protection laws and to stay independent.

Mortgage brokers

Mortgage brokers have operated in the mortgage market for decades. Until recently they acted as link men, helping to bring in deposits for building societies in return for an entitlement to a certain amount which could be channelled to their own customers – people who were looking for loans and were willing to pay premium rates for money, usually to buy property which building societies themselves would not normally consider.

With the end of mortgage rationing the supply of borrowers willing to pay over the odds for difficult-to-get loans has dwindled. There are still borrowers who want a higher percentage advance on a very expensive property or a higher multiple of income than a conventional bank or building society would consider. Borrowers who want to buy property with a sitting tenant may also have to turn to a broker to find a willing lender.

But brokers have found an even more fertile field: shopping around for best buys, offering advice on the growing variety of mortgage packages available and on ways of linking mortgage finance with other financial opportunities. Other activities include speeding up mortgage approvals by helping borrowers to prepare applications and get credit references – as well as finding adventurous lenders for special situations such as property with sitting tenants or short leases, which will revert to the owner of the land in a few years.

They now act as extra eyes and ears for banks and mortgage companies and also for building societies – especially regional societies, who use brokers to place loans in parts of the country where they themselves have few branches. Some of the bigger mortgage brokers also arrange mortgage finance for builders, and some devise loan 'packages', finding institutions willing to put up the money as well as clients to borrow it.

The increase in competition and the entry of new kinds of lender into the housing market encouraged firms providing a range of financial services – investment guidance, insurance broking, tax and pension planning for example – to include mortgage finance as part of their services. Usually they are aimed at sophisticated borrowers looking for large mortgages and often at special rates of interest.

Most of the mortgages brokers offer are endowment or pension mortgages, on which they will receive commission from the lender (so they charge the borrower no fee). Most brokers will also arrange repayment mortgages, for which they will charge the borrower a fee (usually around 0.5 per cent) because they earn no commission. A few brokers, such as Abbeyfield, charge no fee even on repayment mortgages.

But mortgage brokers do not regard themselves as suppliers only of special mortgages, and they offer loans as small as £15,000 or £20,000. Some mortgage brokers claim that at least 10 per cent of all mortgage money (and perhaps as much as 20 per cent) already passes through a broker or financial adviser, and they expect the percentage to rise.

There are several thousand registered mortgage brokers. They range from a large number of local one-man bands to big firms employing dozens of staff. Some of them are independent, others are part of bigger financial conglomerates. The Abaco group owns a number of companies providing financial services, including estate agents. They also own a mortgage broker, John Charcol Ltd, which channels mortgage money for other banks and institutions which have money to lend but no expertise in the mortgage market.

They arrange mortgage packages for builders and developers such as Barratt and Wimpey, and devise new products offering high-percentage advances to borrowers whose income depends heavily on commission income and on bonuses – sources which conventional lenders are reluctant to take into account. They also offer approved borrowers a Mortgage Guarantee Card with a choice of lenders and a range of low-start, fixed-rate and flexible plans.

A number of other brokers have been quick to offer specialized mortgage 'packages' either as a service to existing clients or as a way of bringing in new business. In the summer of 1987, Whitfield & Partners were offering mortgages at 10 per cent interest fixed for two years, switching after that to a variable rate of interest guaranteed to be 0.5 per cent less than the rates charged by the top five building societies. They offered clients guaranteed mortgages of up to 95 per cent of the value of property worth up to £150,000, and 80 per cent on advances in excess of £250,000.

Another broker, Caxtonbrook, offered to find 100 per cent mortgages up to £120,000 and loans as big as four times the main borrower's income plus twice a second income – well above the normal limits of most conventional banks and building societies.

Estate agents

Many estate agents now act as mortgage brokers, and offer to arrange mortgages as well as insurance and other financial services for anyone who buys a home through them. There are more than 16,000 estate agents' offices in Britain. Until very recently they were all local firms, but mergers and takeovers are now common. At least half a dozen national groups have been built up, most of them owned by insurance companies, banks and (most recently) building societies. The big names include the Prudential, Royal Insurance, Lloyds bank, Hambros bank, Abaco financial services group, Hogg Robinson (the insurance broking and travel agency), and a growing number of building societies, including the Nationwide Anglia, the Halifax, the Abbey National, the Bristol & West and the Woolwich. The process is still going on, but there are still over 10,000 independent estate agents.

In the past, many estate agents have acted as agents for a

building society's savings accounts, collecting money and entering receipts in a pass book for investors who couldn't get to a branch office of the building society. In return, the building society paid commission, and perhaps contributed to the upkeep of the estate agent's premises.

The informal link also frequently led building societies to channel some of their loans to the estate agent's clients when mortgages were scarce and led the estate agent to recommend 'their' building society as a lender when funds were flush. But over the last ten years a new generation of estate agents has emerged, actively selling endowment insurance-linked mortgages and earning a valuable extra commission.

The breakdown of the interest-rate cartel, and the arrival on the scene of other lenders offering a variety of mortgage packages and differing interest rates, greatly increased the scope for estate agents to act as mortgage brokers not only for building societies but also for other lenders. Estate agents, insurance companies and the new lenders, including mortgage companies and foreign banks, all began to appreciate the unique opportunities estate agents have to sell mortgages and other financial services as well as houses.

Most home buyers still choose first the house or flat they want to buy and only then think about how to finance it. First-time buyers with no clear idea of what kind of mortgage they want are almost a captive market for a mortgage package once they have decided to buy a particular property – especially if the estate agent can convince them that an endowment mortgage arranged on the spot could clinch a deal and secure the house ahead of other interested buyers.

The insurance operations of estate agents were not effectively regulated at all until the Financial Services Act took effect (in early 1988), forcing them to choose between becoming tied agents for one insurance group or independent advisers pledged to providing customers with 'best advice' on the most suitable mortgage package. The Act applies only to the insurance side of a mortgage however. It does not apply to the mortgage loans, so that tied agents for endowment policies can still offer a choice of lender for the loan itself, and vice versa.

Some estate agents act mainly (if not exclusively) for one

supplier – usually an insurance company which in turn will introduce a lender to provide the mortgage loan. Others, with access to computer screens listing the mortgage packages available to different types of individuals from a selection of lenders, can act as independent brokers, offering home buyers a choice of mortgage quotations.

Some of the bigger chains now owned by banks and building societies have chosen to become independent agents, supplying the owner's mortgages plus a choice of endowment policies while others have opted for the tied route. Most of the estate agencies owned by building societies in fact pre-package their own loans with a range of insurance policies from companies which in the past have produced good bonuses for policy-holders. Black Horse Agencies, owned by Lloyds bank, also offers a choice of lenders as well as a choice of endowment policies, so that customers with established links or loyalties are not obliged to take a Lloyds bank loan.

The Abbey National building society's chain of Cornerstone estate agents, some wholly owned by the society and some owned by franchise holders, have all linked up with Friends' Provident Assurance to provide only Friends' Provident policies. Hambro Countrywide Properties offers mortgage loans supplied by other banks and mortgage companies which have no outlets of their own, but reserves up to 10 per cent of the mortgage lending business it has arranged for its own banking department. The endowment policies and other insurance are provided by a company jointly owned by Hambro Countrywide and Guardian Royal Exchange.

Estate agents owned by insurance companies offer a choice of lenders but the insurance policies are exclusively supplied by the owners. Prudential Property Services, for example, offers only Prudential endowment and other insurance policies, packaged with mortgage loans from a variety of lenders. Royal Insurance and General Accident, the other two companies which were quick to buy up estate agencies, have chosen the same route.

Solicitors

Solicitors have also acted as intermediaries in the past, receiving an unofficial ration of mortgages from friendly building societies in return for channelling clients' savings into the local branch of the society. The abolition of restrictions on solicitors' advertising means that they can publicize their services, and some now offer to find mortgages as well as to provide cheap conveyancing and other legal services.

Builders

Most of the leading building firms also now offer mortgage finance as part of the package to help sell new homes. National builders such as Wimpey, Barratt and Ideal Homes have arrangements with mortgage companies and brokers to provide mortgage loans. In many cases they offer 100 per cent mortgages. Local builders often have arrangements with local building societies to supply mortgages.

Builders may subsidize mortgage rates for a year or more to make the package attractive, and include carpets, curtains and kitchen equipment in the deal. Ideal Homes, for example, has been offering 100 per cent mortgages, a £750 cash rebate and interest-free loans of up to £1,500 for three years to help with buyers' costs. Wimpey has been offering 100 per cent mortgages, interest-rate subsidies for up to three years, cash rebates of up to £1,440 for early completion of purchase and a Home Exchange scheme to buy customers' existing homes. But builders' packages are not always the best in the long run, and the endowment policies they offer are not always obtained from insurance companies with the best investment track record.

6
Mortgages explained

Mortgage loans are mainly used to help borrowers buy property, although they can also be used to finance home improvements, and nowadays for other purposes as well. In all cases, however, the property is pledged as security to guarantee that the loan will be repaid. The borrower is known in law as the mortgagor – it is actually the borrower who gives a mortgage as security when he or she borrows money from the lender, or mortgagee. The property legally belongs to the borrower. The borrower can decide to sell or keep it, and the borrower enjoys the benefit if its value goes up and suffers the loss if it goes down.

But the borrower is obliged to pay interest on time and to repay the loan, and the lender can claim the property and sell it to redeem the debt if the borrower fails to pay up.

Mortgages are intended to be repaid over a fixed period of time which is agreed in advance. The normal term is 20, 25 or 30 years, although special arrangements may be necessary for older borrowers (see Chapter 12) and in some cases it may be possible for young borrowers with excellent financial prospects to take out a mortgage for as long as 40 years.

The borrower can pay off the mortgage debt at any time (though some lenders require borrowers to pay an extra three months' interest if they wish to pay the debt off early) and the average life of a mortgage has been declining steadily as families move house more frequently. It is now down to about five or six years on average, even less in London and the south-east, where the housing market is active and individuals are highly mobile.

The rate of interest to be charged on a mortgage has to be advertised in advance. Some lenders now offer rates of interest which are fixed for a limited period, usually one or two years. But banks and building societies themselves have to pay competitive rates of interest to borrow the money they relend, and to pass on costs as well as benefits to borrowers. Commercial interest rates can rise and fall several percentage points within a matter of weeks, so the majority of mortgages are and will continue to be subject to change at short notice. Some lenders change rates for new business immediately, and new rates for existing loans usually take effect at the end of the month in which the charge is announced.

Repayment mortgages

Competition has produced a growing number of variations on the mortgage theme. The annuity or repayment mortgage was until recently much the most common type – as recently as 1982, three-quarters of all mortgages were repayment mortgages – but the proportion has now fallen to around 30 per cent of all new loans. With a repayment mortgage, borrowers agree to pay equal instalments at regular intervals, usually every month, over the agreed life of the loan. Each instalment consists of an interest payment and some repayment of the capital amount borrowed.

The monthly repayments depend on the gross interest rate charged by the lender, the basic rate of tax relief due to the borrower, and the period of repayment – the longer the loan, the larger the total interest which has to be paid on the amount borrowed, but the lower the monthly instalments, because the capital is being repaid more slowly. For example, with an interest rate of 10 per cent and tax relief at 25p on each pound of interest, the payments on a £20,000 mortgage being repaid in equal net monthly instalments over a period of 20 years will be £163.49 a month, making a total of £39,238. If repayment is made over 25 years the monthly payment falls to £149.52, because capital is being repaid more slowly, but the total paid rises to £44,856. And over a 30-year mortgage the monthly payment drops to £141.12 but the total paid rises to £50,803.

Higher-rate taxpayers get an even better deal after allowing for tax relief, although they can get relief on the interest only up to the current ceiling (£30,000 in 1988–89) and they have to earn enough at the higher rate to get full relief at that rate. Mortgage payments allow for only the basic-rate tax relief, and higher-rate taxpayers have to claim the extra relief through a reduction in the income tax they pay. On the same £20,000 mortgage outlined above, someone subject to income tax at 40 per cent would pay the same amount of interest and could claim an extra £16.03 a month over 20 years, or an extra £16.57 a month over 25 years. (That assumes that he or she earns enough income at the higher rate for all the interest due to be paid out of that high-rate income. For example, a taxpayer whose gross interest payment is £3,000 a year must earn at least £3,000 taxed at the higher rate to qualify for full tax relief at the higher rate. If for example he or she earns only £2,000 taxable at the higher rate, the remaining £1,000 of interest qualifies only for tax relief at a lower rate.)

Table 9 shows the effect of a borrower's rate of income tax on net mortgage payments, and how borrowers over a longer period pay less each month but more in total than borrowers with a shorter mortgage agreement.

In the early years of a repayment mortgage, interest will swallow up most of the monthly payments and the capital sum still owed will reduce only slowly. But as time goes by the interest due on the remaining capital declines and the capital can be paid off faster. On a standard 25-year mortgage loan, interest will account for roughly 90 per cent of the monthly

Table 9
Net cost of a repayment mortgage

Income tax rate	Payment (£) over 20 years monthly	total	Payment (£) over 25 years monthly	total	Payment (£) over 30 years monthly	total
25%	163.60	39,264	149.60	44,880	141.20	50,832
40%	145.40	34,896	130.40	39,120	121.20	43,632

The figures apply to a £20,000 mortgage at 10% gross interest. They show costs after all tax relief has been taken into account. Monthly payments to the lender will be higher if higher-rate tax is involved, because MIRAS gives relief at only the basic rate of tax.

payment in the first year, falling to around 80 per cent after 5 years, 70 per cent after 10 years, under 60 per cent after 15 years, under 40 per cent after 20 years and about 10 per cent in the final year.

Gross and net profiles

Until 1983, borrowers made their mortgage payments to the lenders in full, and got their tax relief from the Inland Revenue by claiming higher tax allowances and so paying reduced income tax. Lenders calculated equal monthly payments needed to pay off the mortgage without regard to tax relief. But with a repayment mortgage the amount of income tax relief allowed gradually decreases over the years as the interest element in the monthly mortgage payments decreases – so the net monthly cost to the borrower started low and actually increased as the years passed.

With the switch to giving mortgage tax relief at source, working out payments in the same way would also require the borrower to pay an increasing amount each year to the lender, as capital is repaid and the amount of interest (and therefore tax relief) is reduced. Most banks and some building societies still allow borrowers to make payments in this way, so as to take advantage of full tax relief on the interest and to keep the monthly payments down in the early years. But this method, known as the gross profile or increasing net method of calculating payments, is now less common. (Although it is called a *gross* profile repayment, the name refers only to the way the repayments are calculated. Interest is still normally paid *net*, ie after deducting tax relief.)

The alternative, which is applied to practically all borrowers who do not ask for a gross profile mortgage, is to calculate level monthly repayments *after* allowing for tax relief. This is known as the net profile or constant net method of payment.

The effect of using the net profile rather than the gross profile method is to increase the net amount borrowers have to pay in the early years; this speeds up capital repayments and so reduces the total amount of interest the borrower has to pay over the full life of the mortgage. Working out the monthly amount required to give a constant net payment is a rather complicated calculation which cannot be done on the back of an envelope. But roughly, first-year payments are increased by about 6 per cent, while payments in the second half of the mortgage are reduced by as much as 10–15 per cent.

The effect can be seen in Table 10. With a gross profile repayment mortgage, the combined total each month of capital repaid, net interest paid and tax relief received is constant throughout the life of the mortgage – although the proportions of each will change each year. With a net profile mortgage, the combined total each month of capital repaid and net interest paid is flat throughout, but the tax relief diminishes. Moving from gross to net profile involves *raising* the combined total of capital and net interest at the start and lowering it at the end of the mortgage period. The increase in early payments consists entirely of capital, however, which speeds up repayment and reduces the total interest payable.

The figures in Table 10 assume that interest rates and income tax rates are unchanged throughout the life of a mortgage. If these rates change, the lenders have to recalculate the repayments and notify all borrowers of the new net amount they should pay each month.

Table 10
Gross and net profile payments compared

After year	Gross profile Net yearly payment (£)	Still owing (£)	Net profile Net yearly payment (£)	Still owing (£)
1	91.24	991.26	95.69	986.81
5	92.37	945.57	95.69	922.25
10	94.64	853.85	95.69	806.68
15	98.47	699.29	95.69	634.89
20	104.93	438.85	95.69	379.55
25	115.80	NIL	95.69	NIL

Total net interest paid: gross profile £1,476.37, net profile £1,392.25.
Figures are for a £1,000 mortgage at 11% gross interest.

Interest rate changes

A change in mortgage interest rates alters the monthly payments needed to pay off a repayment mortgage but the effects are partly offset by a change in the capital repayments. A cut in interest rates reduces the interest payment but part of the benefit is used to accelerate repayments, while a rise in interest rates is partly offset by cutting the repayments. The precise amount of the change will depend on the rate of tax relief, on how long the mortgage has been running and on how much capital has already been repaid. The effects of a change in interest rates will also be slightly greater on a gross profile mortgage than on a net profile mortgage, because the interest element is greater in the early years of a gross profile mortgage and less in the later years.

A borrower who has a net profile or constant net repayment mortgage of £30,000, being paid back over 25 years at 9 per cent interest before tax, would have to pay £209.72 each month, after tax relief at a basic rate of 25p in the pound. If the rate rises to 10 per cent during the second year of the mortgage the monthly payments will go up from £209.72 to £223.90 each month. If there are no other changes in rates, that figure will continue to apply until the mortgage has been paid off.

If the rate goes up to 10 per cent when the mortgage is already in its fifth year, however, the monthly payments would go up from £209.72 to £222.67, because the interest element in the payment will by then have decreased. Payments on a similar mortgage in its tenth year would go up from £209.72 to £220.35 in response to the same interest rate change, in the fifteenth year to £217.67, in the twentieth year to £214.62; in the final year of a 25-year mortgage the same change would put the payments up to £211.19, an increase of just £1.47.

On a gross profile repayment mortgage in the same circumstances, the monthly payments after tax relief would rise gradually each year from £198.93 a month in the second year to £206.91 a month in the tenth year and £249.26 a month in the final year, even if the interest rate stays at 9 per cent, because of the way the payments are structured. A rise in the interest rate to 10 per cent would put up the payments from £198.93 to £213.20 a month if the mortgage is in its second year. If the mortgage is in its fifth year the payments would go up from £201.30 to £214.33 a month, in the fifteenth year from £215.55 to £223.37 and in the final year from £249.26 to £256.85, an increase of £7.59 a month.

If the rate goes up from 10 per cent to 11 per cent the effects on repayments will be slightly greater than on a change from 9 to 10 per cent. If rates decrease, the effects of a 1 per cent change will be slightly less.

Tax changes

Changes in the rates of income tax also automatically affect monthly payments by altering the amount of tax relief. A cut in the basic rate of tax reduces the amount of tax relief and therefore *increases* the net payments required. In the simplest case, when the mortgage interest rate is 10 per cent gross and the basic rate of income tax is 25 per cent, the net rate is $10 \times (100 - 25)/100 = 7.5$ per cent. If the basic rate goes down to 24p the net rate goes up to $10 \times (100 - 24)/100 = 7.6$ per cent. Reducing the basic rate of tax to 23p would bring the net rate of interest payable up to $10 \times (100 - 23)/100 = 7.7$ per cent and so on. Reductions in the higher rates of tax will also reduce the benefits of higher-rate tax relief and raise the net rate of interest the borrower is paying.

With a repayment mortgage, the effect of a tax change declines with the age of the loan. In the first year, a change of 1p in the pound in the basic rate of tax will alter the repayments by about £12 a year for each £10,000 of loan. A 10p change in the top rate of tax would alter the annual payment by about £114 a year. The effect diminishes as the interest element in the payments declines, to about £7 a year by year ten.

Annual adjustments

The MIRAS system means that banks and building societies act as unofficial civil servants whenever income tax rates change. Some lenders have tried in recent years to cut down the paperwork involved by adjusting interest rates whenever necessary but requiring borrowers to change their monthly payments or standing orders only once a year. This delays the impact of rising rates but is understandably not very popular with borrowers when mortgage rates are coming down and they want to enjoy the benefit immediately. Most lenders still calculate the new monthly repayment due and send out notices to every borrower every time mortgage interest rates or income tax rates change.

Extended payments

In 1973–74 and again in 1980, mortgage interest rates rose steeply immediately after a steep rise in house prices, and many first-time buyers who had been forced to borrow heavily to get on to the housing ladder were unable to meet the increased payments. The building societies, who dominated the mortgage market at the time, had little choice but to let borrowers pay less than the full amount due and to extend the life of the mortgage. If the mortgage rate is at 10 per cent every one per cent extra on the interest rate lengthens the life of a new repayment mortgage by as much as six years if the borrower fails to make the extra payment.

Some borrowers were allowed to pay only the interest on their mortgages and postpone all repayments of capital, lengthening the life of their mortgages to infinity. It is not a policy to be recommended.

When interest rates fall, borrowers are able to start paying off capital again by keeping their monthly payments unchanged, and the life of their mortgages shortens again. It does not, of course, go back to its original finishing date; borrowers found the big disadvantage of failing to keep up payments was that they could no longer keep a check on the date when they would have paid off their mortgage. But the ability to hold payments down and extend the life of the mortgage was one of the main attractions of a repayment mortgage.

Too many borrowers took advantage of the concession, however. Some failed to raise their payments at all, and let their mortgages grow larger while using the money they saved for other purposes. As a result some societies – including the biggest lender, the Halifax building society – now insist that borrowers must pay any increase in interest charges in full, and stick strictly to the agreed repayment terms.

Repayment mortgages cannot be transferred from one property to another. If the borrower decides to move, he or she has to pay off the mortgage and take out a new one on the next property. Any profit on the sale, after the original mortgage has been paid back, goes to the borrower in cash. Until recently, the bank or building society which provided the mortgage on the borrower's next home would usually insist on the profit being reinvested. Someone who sold a house for £90,000 and paid off a £40,000 mortgage would be expected to put at least £45,000 into the next home. But competition has now forced lenders to be more flexible: many borrowers are able to take more of the profit out as a tax-free gain and take out a bigger loan on the next house.

Insurance policies

A repayment mortgage is a straightforward loan, with no extra charges. But borrowers are urged to have a life insurance policy which will guarantee enough money to redeem the mortgage in full if the borrower dies before it has been repaid. Such a policy is obviously desirable if the borrower has a family who could not afford to maintain the payments on their own. Most insurance companies offer a choice of policy. A **decreasing term** policy provides cover which is highest in the early years and gradually decreases with time as the mortgage is paid off and the capital owed to the lender diminishes. **Level term** insurance guarantees to pay out a sum equal to the original mortgage if the borrower dies at any stage during the life of the

Table 11
Monthly cost of decreasing term life insurance

Starting age	Smoker's premium (£)		Non-smoker's premium (£)	
	Male	Female	Male	Female
25	3.60	3.30	3.30	3.00
30	4.80	3.90	3.90	3.30
35	7.20	5.70	5.70	4.50
40	12.00	8.70	8.70	6.60

Table applies to a £30,000 repayment mortgage over 25 years.
Source Norwich Union

mortgage. The amount of the insurance premium which the borrower has to pay depends on the borrower's age and life expectancy, but a decreasing term policy will naturally be cheaper than a level term policy.

Most lenders also require buyers who want to borrow more than 75 per cent of the value of a property to take out additional insurance, called a mortgage indemnity policy, to insure against being unable to repay the loan. The premium is usually a one-off payment of about £3 per £1,000 borrowed in excess of the specified level.

Endowment mortgages

Some form of insurance cover is desirable to protect the borrower's dependants. One answer to the problem is an endowment mortgage, which combines a mortgage loan from the lender with an insurance policy from one of the leading life insurance companies.

With an endowment mortgage, the borrower pays to the lender only the interest on the capital borrowed. The rest of the monthly payment consists of an insurance premium which goes separately to the insurance company. The premium is invested in an endowment insurance policy which pays out if the borrower dies or on the day the mortgage is due to be repaid, whichever is the earlier. The amount of the insurance premium depends on how old the borrower is when he or she takes out the mortgage – the younger the borrower, the smaller the premium will be.

Endowment mortgages were originally intended just to provide the minimum level of life insurance – just enough cover to pay off the mortgage if the borrower died before completing the payments and just enough to pay it off if the borrower lived. The insurance premium for this kind of 'without profits' policy was roughly the same as the capital payments on a repayment mortgage, and there was not much to choose between them.

Non-profit endowment mortgages are still available. Borrowers who need a second mortgage or a top-up loan to help them buy a property sometimes still find that lenders will insist that borrowers take out non-profit policies in order to guarantee repayment of the extra loan if the borrower dies. But very few borrowers would nowadays choose an endowment policy without profits.

With-profits policies

Policies which earn bonuses and profits are much more attractive. Bonuses and profits were not easy to earn in the 1940s and 1950s, when interest rates and dividends were low. But high rates of inflation during the 1960s and 1970s reduced the real value of the mortgage by the time it was repaid, and high interest rates meant that the insurance companies could provide substantial bonuses in addition to repaying the mortgage. In the 1980s, inflation has slowed down but insurance companies have still found it possible to declare good bonuses from the investment of the premiums paid for endowment policies.

Insurers have been able to offer 'with-profits' endowment policies that provide life insurance cover in case the borrower dies before paying the mortgage off, plus enough money to pay off the mortgage when it matures, *and* offer borrowers a tax-free bonus as well. The premiums are invested by the insurance company and earn annual bonuses, declared each year. They usually average perhaps 5 per cent of the with-profit endowment sum insured and once declared they are guaranteed. When the mortgage and the policy mature, the insurance company also adds on a terminal bonus paid out of accumulated profits. The size of this terminal bonus depends on how well the premiums have been invested over the life of the policy. It is often as big as all the accumulated annual bonuses, but of course it is not guaranteed and could be much less.

The premiums on a with-profits endowment policy make the net monthly payments about 20 per cent higher than on a repayment mortgage. But as long ago as 1967 the Low-Cost Endowment policy was developed as a kind of half-way house. By the mid-1970s, a growing number of insurance companies were offering them, and they are now by far the most popular type of endowment policy.

Low-cost endowment mortgages

Low-cost endowment policies provide a mixture of with-profit endowment and straightforward temporary life insurance. The premiums are lower than on a with-profits endowment policy for the full amount of the mortgage because it is assumed that a certain level of bonuses will be declared and used to pay off part of the mortgage. So the monthly costs of a low-cost endowment mortgage are roughly the same as on a repayment mortgage.

Over a 10-year period, for example, the policy has only a short time to earn bonuses. So between 67 per cent and 70 per cent of the loan is repaid from the guaranteed with-profit endowment sum insured, and 30–33 per cent is repaid from the bonuses. Longer-term loans have longer to accumulate bonuses so the proportion of mortgage repaid from the guaranteed with-profit endowment sum insured on a typical 25-year low-cost endowment policy falls to 35–38 per cent and the 62–65 per cent is required from bonuses.

The annual bonuses and the terminal bonus will be smaller than those produced by a full with-profits policy, and low-cost endowment policies do not guarantee unconditionally to pay off the mortgage in full when they mature. But most insurance companies set the monthly premiums payable so that the policy should pay off the mortgage in full even if they declare only 80 per cent of those which would be projected if current annual bonus rates continue and no terminal bonuses are paid. In recent years even the worst-invested endowment policies have earned more than enough to redeem the mortgage. But if the economy did deteriorate very drastically in future, and bonuses did not add up to enough to pay off the mortgage, the borrower would have to find the difference.

No capital at all is paid off until an endowment mortgage reaches the end of the agreed period. The borrower pays interest on the full amount of the loan from start to finish, and will inevitably pay more interest over the life of the mortgage than someone borrowing the same amount on a repayment mortgage.

The extra interest qualifies for tax relief, but with mortgage interest at 10 per cent gross and 7.5 per cent net the net interest alone after tax relief at the basic rate on a £30,000 endowment mortgage repaid after 20 years will be £45,000; after 25 years it would be £56,250, and after 30 years £67,500. By comparison, the interest on a repayment mortgage would be £28,855 over 20 years, £37,284 over 25 years and £46,205 over 30 years.

But the borrower with a repayment mortgage is paying back his £30,000 as well, while the endowment policy-holder is paying insurance premiums which are being invested to produce a capital sum which should not only pay off the mortgage but also produce a tax-free bonus – because the life office is able to earn interest on the premiums to offset extra interest paid on the mortgage.

The combined net cost of a low-cost endowment policy, including interest, investment premiums and built-in life insurance cover, will be roughly the same as the net cost of a repayment mortgage, including interest, the capital repayments and the extra cost of basic life insurance. But the 'profile' of the payments on an endowment policy is different.

The interest payments on an endowment mortgage vary with the current mortgage rate of course, but the monthly endowment policy premium payment is decided at the start of the mortgage and does not change. It does, however, depend on how old the borrower is when the policy is taken out, on whether the borrower is a man, a woman or a couple taking out a joint mortgage, and on how long the mortgage is intended to last.

Table 12
Monthly endowment premiums

Age next birthday	Monthly premium (£)		
	Male	Female	Couple
25	£37.20	£37.20	£39.00
30	£38.10	£37.50	£39.90
35	£39.60	£38.70	£42.60
40	£43.50	£41.10	£47.70
45	£50.70	£45.00	£57.60

Table assumes a £30,000 mortgage over 25 years. Premiums include a monthly policy fee of £1.20.
Source Norwich Union

The younger the borrower when the mortgage is started, the lower the monthly premium will be. A man aged 25 next birthday would pay about £37.20 a month on a £30,000 low-cost endowment mortgage over 25 years. A woman borrower would pay the same, and a couple taking out a joint mortgage would expect to pay about £39 a month if they are both 25 next birthday.

A man aged 30 next birthday would pay £38.10 a month, a woman only £37.50 and a couple £39.90. Coming up to 40 at the start of a low-cost endowment mortgage, a man would pay £43.50 a month, a woman £41.10 and a couple £47.70. Rates then rise faster with the age of the borrower at the start of the mortgage, and a man aged 50 next birthday would pay £63.70 a month for the same 25-year mortgage.

The length of the mortgage also has an effect on the endowment premium the borrower is expected to pay. The longer the mortgage, the lower the monthly premiums will be, because the insurance company has longer to invest the premiums and accumulate enough to pay the mortgage off – and this more than compensates for the increased risk of the borrower dying before making all the payments (at least for the average borrower).

A man aged 30 next birthday taking out a low-cost endowment mortgage for 20 years would have to pay £58.20 a month, but over a 25-year period the same policy for the same man would cost only £38.10 a month, over 30 years only £26.40 a month and over 35 years just £19.80 a month.

Repayment versus low-cost endowment

Because the components of a repayment and an endowment mortgage are different it is not easy to make a strict comparison between them. Excluding any life insurance premiums at 10.25% interest, it can be seen in Table 13 that the net cost of a repayment mortgage will be slightly lower than the net cost of a low-cost endowment policy and the advantage will grow fractionally over a longer-term mortgage. But even over a 35-year mortgage a 30-year-old borrower will be saving only about £4.25 a month on a monthly payment of just over £200 by having a repayment mortgage, and over a normal 25-year term the advantage is £2.31 a month.

If allowance is made for a temporary life insurance policy to guarantee repayment of the loan if the borrower dies, the advantage swings marginally in favour of the low-cost endowment policy, especially over a shorter-term mortgage of 20 or 25 years – but once again the difference is fractional. Age makes very little difference if allowance is made for life insurance with a repayment mortgage. At lower interest rates the initial cost comparison increasing favours low cost endowment, whereas with higher interest rates the reverse is true.

Advantages of endowments

The great attraction of an endowment policy in recent years, however, has been the prospect of not just paying off the mortgage, but of also enjoying an additional tax-free lump sum. Bonuses which provide this additional amount are not guaranteed, of course, and indeed a low-cost endowment policy will not actually guarantee to pay off the mortgage, if the investments fail to accumulate the expected return. But most insurance companies fix the level of premiums so that they will cover the mortgage if they earn an annual return of about 8–8.5 per cent after tax, and they have done substantially better than that in recent years.

Table 13
Net costs of low-cost endowment and repayment mortgages

| | Monthly payments (£) | | | | | |
| | Endowment mortgage | | | Repayment mortgage | | |
	Interest	Premium	Total	Interest and capital	Temporary life cover	Total
Over 20 years	192.19	58.20	250.39	248.74	3.30	252.04
Over 25 years	192.19	38.10	230.29	227.98	3.90	231.88
Over 30 years	192.19	26.40	218.59	215.55	4.80	220.35
Over 35 years	192.19	19.80	211.99	207.74	6.00	213.74

Figures are for a £30,000 mortgage at 10.25% gross interest, and assume the borrower is a 30-year-old male.

Disadvantages of endowments

Unlike a repayment mortgage without life insurance, an endowment mortgage becomes more expensive the older the borrower is when the mortgage is taken out. A man aged 35 when he takes out a £30,000 mortgage and a 25-year policy would expect to pay about £450 more during the 25-year period than a 30-year old. The extra cost rises to £1,620 if he starts at age 40, and £6,120 if he starts at 50. Borrowers with a history of ill health or a known medical condition will also be expected to pay higher premiums than the average for their age, and in some cases endowment mortgages could be expensive, but for some borrowers' families the life insurance will be important despite this additional outlay.

A borrower with an endowment mortgage does not have the option to delay the date on which the mortgage is repaid and reduce the endowment premiums without the agreement of the lender and the insurance company. The borrower can transfer an endowment policy from one mortgage to the next. But if he or she sells the property the borrower can take the money in full only by paying off the mortgage and surrendering the policy for its current surrender value; if the policy has been going for less than about five years this will usually be less than the premiums that have been paid.

Transferability

Borrowers who want to borrow more to finance a move up-market will need a bigger and probably a longer loan. At one time, some brokers and agents would also try to persuade endowment policy-holders to redeem their original policies when they moved house, and to take out a new one with an insurance company chosen by the broker, who earned commission on the deal. Cashing in a policy is not normally a good idea, however, unless the policy is earning very poor bonuses. It normally pays to keep the original policy, especially if it was taken out before 13 March 1984, in which case the policy qualifies for some tax relief on the premiums, as well as on the interest on the loan.

The original policy may not have earned enough bonuses to cover a larger mortgage on a move to a more expensive home, and will generally mature too early to cover the mortgage repayment if the borrower wants to repay over a longer period. Borrowers will therefore need some extra cover. Most insurance companies will allow borrowers to increase their cover without having a fresh medical examination, and many will allow policies to be extended if the change does not take the borrower past the age of 65 or 70. But some companies are less flexible. In these cases, the borrower will need to take out a new endowment policy to cover the difference between the value of the existing policy and the total of the new loan, and to cover the whole period until the new mortgage is to be paid off. When the original policy matures, it pays off part of the mortgage, interest payments reduce and only the additional policy continues, to pay off the balance when it too matures.

Home owners with an endowment mortgage usually go back to their original lender when they move home, and take out an additional endowment policy with the same insurance company. But they are not under any obligation to do so. In the past, some lenders were reluctant to accept policies from some other insurance companies with whom they did not normally deal as security for a mortgage loan, and borrowers sometimes felt pressured to cash in old policies and start again when they moved. Others may have felt deterred from moving, or under an obligation to go back to the original lender, even when cheaper mortgage packages were available elsewhere.

But, by 1987, 18 out of the top 20 building societies were willing to accept existing endowment policies from any of the leading insurance companies as full or part security for a loan. The Financial Services Act obliges independent brokers, including most building societies, to offer borrowers 'best advice'. That effectively guarantees borrowers the right to mix existing policies and new policies when taking out a new mortgage, and gives them freedom to change lenders without losing the accumulated value of existing policies.

The swing to endowments

The balance of advantage between repayment and endowment mortgages has shifted in recent years. Until 1984, the insurance premiums as well as the interest paid on endowment mortgages qualified for tax relief. The borrower could reclaim only 15 per cent of the premium against tax, but it was enough to make endowment mortgages attractive, especially to higher-rate taxpayers. The advantage was offset, however, by the building societies' habit of charging higher interest rates on endowment mortgages – usually 0.5 per cent above the current rate on repayment mortgages – as well as taking a commission fee from the insurance company.

Higher interest rates made endowment mortgages slightly more expensive than the equivalent repayment mortgage, even after allowing for tax relief, and endowment mortgages made up rather less than a quarter of the total mortgage market during the 1970s. But the rise in real interest rates and dividends, and the capital gains which insurance companies were able to earn from 1980 onwards, made the prospect of a tax-free lump sum increasingly attractive. As building societies became increasingly competitive they also began to favour endowment mortgages because of the opportunities to earn commission from the insurance companies.

The Chancellor's decision in March 1983 to switch the system of tax relief to MIRAS changed the system of claiming tax relief, and the resulting switch from gross profile repayments to net profile repayments effectively raised the monthly payments required in the early years of a repayment mortgage by about 50p per £1,000, making them slightly more expensive than endowment mortgages for most borrowers.

Endowment mortgages continued to qualify for tax relief on the premiums and the combination of events made the attractions of endowment mortgages much more obvious to borrowers. From just 20 per cent of the mortgage market in 1982 endowment mortgages jumped to 32 per cent in the first quarter of 1983, 56 per cent in the second quarter and rose to a peak of 68 per cent in the first quarter of 1984.

In the 1984 Budget the Chancellor abolished tax relief on all new insurance policies, including endowment policies, with effect from 13 March, although existing policies continue to qualify until they mature. The loss of tax relief on the premiums cut endowment policies' share of the market back again to around 55 per cent in 1984 and 1985. But the continuing high level of interest rates and a rising stock market allowed insurance companies to reduce their premiums and still offer increasingly tempting annual and terminal bonuses which offset the loss of tax relief on new policies.

Insurance companies have done so well with their investments over the last 10 years that they could pull in business with the prospect of huge bonuses in future simply by making compound projections of recent gains over the next 20 or 30 years. But continuous growth at such rates is unrealistic, and in 1986 the companies, through their trade association, agreed to stop projecting continuing bonus rates and to show a more cautious view of investment income and profits over a period of 20 to 30 years by assuming an annual return of 10.75 per cent. But rapid economic growth still allows most lenders to project additional lump sums on 25-year low-cost endowment policies of around 50 per cent of the capital borrowed – enough to keep the balance of advantage in favour of endowments even if inflation has reduced the value of the bonus by the time it arrives.

Lenders continued to charge higher interest rates on endowment mortgages until early 1986. Lloyds bank then decided to abolish differential interest rates and most other lenders were quickly forced to do the same, giving endowment mortgages even greater advantages. Only a handful of lenders (the Loughborough building society, the Penrith, the Essex Equitable, the Hampshire, the Hanley Permanent and the Harpenden) still charged a higher interest on endowment mortgages in 1987, but some lenders (the TSB, the NHLC and the Manchester building society) now charge higher rates on repayment mortgages.

Endowment mortgages have also been made increasingly adaptable, so as to attract borrowers. Building societies and banks have become increasingly conscious of the opportunity for earning commission on the insurance premiums. By 1987, more than two-thirds of all new mortgages were linked to endowment policies. Many building societies and banks have also written to holders of repayment mortgages drawing their attention to the ending of the interest-rate differential and the opportunities with endowments for earning tax-free bonuses when the mortgages are paid off, and inviting them to switch their mortgages.

Unit-linked mortgages

The investment performance of conventional endowment mortgages is based on a policy of investing premiums in a broadly based fund of shares, property and fixed interest securities.

But the consistent rapid rise in stock market values during the 1980s encouraged a number of insurance companies to offer the prospect of even bigger payouts, based on more adventurous investment of the premiums. Linking mortgages to individual shares was still considered too risky, but unit-linked policies which contain shares in a variety of different companies in order to spread the risks, seemed ideal. In June 1982, Abbey Life introduced Mortgage Master – the first mortgage to be backed by a policy with the premiums invested in a unit-linked insurance, managed by Abbey Life's own investment managers.

The stock market continued to rise, most unit-linked policies performed well and five years later more than 40 insurance companies were offering unit-linked policies to go with mortgages. The monthly contributions are roughly similar to endowment premiums. Most of the companies are relative newcomers on the insurance scene, including M & G, Allied Dunbar, Target and Black Horse Life as well as Abbey Life, but many of the old insurance companies – including Legal & General, Guardian Royal Exchange, Cannon Insurance, Equitable Insurance, Norwich Union, Sun Life and Sun Life of Canada – also offer policies invested in selected unit trusts.

A borrower taking out a unit-linked mortgage pays interest on the loan to the lender, and a monthly premium to an insurance company in the same way as on an endowment mortgage. Part of the premium is used to provide life insurance, to pay off either a set sum to redeem the mortgage or the difference between the value of the units in the fund and the amount of the loan if the borrower dies.

Some of the premium is used to pay charges and the balance is invested in units in one or more unit trusts. Most insurance companies assume the premiums invested will grow in value by 7.5 per cent a year, and fix the premiums so that they will provide enough money to pay the mortgage off in full if they earn that rate of return.

Borrowers are kept informed of how many units have been bought and in which fund, so they can watch their current value in the financial pages of the newspapers.

Like an endowment policy a unit-linked scheme does not usually guarantee to pay the mortgage loan off, and if the units fail to meet the 7.5 per cent growth target over a number of years the borrower will be asked to contribute more each month or to prolong the payment period.

Most unit-linked mortgage payments have been invested in units selected by the insurance company itself. But by 1987 some companies, for example the Scottish Mutual, were offering investors a choice of investing in three or four different unit-linked funds managed by the Scottish Mutual's investment managers – categorized as 'safe', 'steady' or a slightly more speculative 'high growth', with the right to switch from one to another, initially without charge.

Unit-linked investments are not cheap, however. There is often a price spread of about 5 per cent between the price at which investors buy units and the price at which they sell. There is also a yearly management charge of about 0.75 per cent which has to be paid on all money invested in unit trusts, and an annual policy fee to pay.

Unit-linked mortgages have not been in existence long enough to predict how well they will compare with endowment mortgages over 20–25 years or more. But unit-linked investment schemes have been available for many years and they have outperformed conventional with-profits endowment policies over the last 10, 15 and 20 years. According to *Planned Savings* magazine in February 1987, the average unit-linked fund had outperformed the average with-profits endowment policy by between 30 and 50 per cent over all three periods.

Unit-linked policies have been more successful because most of the money has been invested in shares rather than in a mixture of shares and government securities. But unit-linked policies, like shares, can also go down in value as well as up. The value of the units in most unit-linked policies fell by 30 per cent in three weeks during the stock market crash in October 1987.

Some unit-linked policies – such as Guardian Royal Exchange's Homebuilder, which is claimed to be the market leader – do guarantee to earn enough profit to redeem the mortgage and show a surplus, but they assume a lower return on the units, so the monthly premiums are higher. Most unit-linked schemes do not offer a guarantee, but they do monitor the value of the units, and if they failed to grow fast enough investors could be called upon to increase their contributions or to extend the length of their mortgage and go on paying premiums and interest until the units are worth enough to redeem the mortgage.

Fortunately this is unlikely to happen. But unit-linked policies *are* likely to vary much more in value than ordinary endowment policies which are more widely invested and have annual guaranteed bonuses. Getting the timing right when the policy matures is also very important. Long before the mortgage is due to be repaid, the market could be buoyant and the policy could be worth more than enough to cover the loan; but by the time the repayment is required the stock market could be depressed and the units worth much less. Borrowers with unit-linked policies do therefore have the right to repay their mortgages early. The investment managers also have a duty to advise holders of unit-linked mortgages when early repayment could be beneficial, and some switch to a conventional endowment policy for the last few years. When the mortgage is paid off some companies have encouraged unit-linked mortgage holders to retain the surplus units and keep the policy going as an investment – although most have a maximum life for a policy and a maximum age for the policy-holder.

Avon Insurance in 1986 devised a further variation on a unit-linked policy, diverting up to £18 a month of the premiums into a tax-exempt fund run by the Lancashire & Yorkshire Friendly Society. The tax advantages reduce the premium by about £5 a month on a £30,000 mortgage and increase the projected surplus after 25 years by an assumed £4,000.

Borrowers who take out unit-linked mortgages can switch them from one home to the next like an endowment mortgage whenever they want to move, topping up the scheme by increasing the premiums if necessary to support a bigger mortgage loan. But unit-linked mortgages may be less easy to transfer from one lender to another if borrowers do want to move or to remortgage their home. At the end of 1987 there were still half a dozen building societies, including the Leeds, which did not lend money against unit-linked policies because the value of the units is liable to fluctuate. Borrowers with unit-linked mortgages also have life insurance built in to pay off the mortgage if they die before the units are worth enough to do so. They also need mortgage indemnity policies if they want to borrow more than 75–80 per cent of the property value.

Pension mortgages

The loss of tax relief on endowment mortgage premiums has increased the attractions of pension mortgages. As with endowments, the borrower pays only interest to the lender; to provide for repayment of the capital, the borrower contributes to a pension fund run by an insurance company. The pension scheme is accepted by the mortgage lender as security for a mortgage loan. When it matures the pension plan provides a tax-free lump sum to pay off the mortgage as well as a (taxable) annual pension in retirement.

The size of the mortgage is linked to the size of the lump sum the pension is expected to produce. Some lenders will advance up to 100 per cent of the projected lump sum, others limit loans to about 80 per cent of it. Unlike endowment policies, pension plans cannot be assigned to a third party, so borrowers must also have a separate life insurance policy as security in the event of their death, and most lenders also require borrowers to have a mortgage indemnity policy if the loan exceeds 75–80 per cent of the property's value.

Unlike insurance premiums, pension fund contributions still qualify for tax relief. But until recently relatively few borrowers have been eligible for pension mortgages because in practice they were available only to certain groups – executives who qualified for special 'Top Hat' company pension schemes, individuals who were self-employed and people who worked for companies which did not offer a company pension scheme. As an additional disadvantage, the Inland Revenue did not allow individuals in normal occupations to retire and take a lump sum before they reached the age of 60. This rule effectively meant borrowers had to be at least 35 before they could take out a 25-year pension mortgage.

The scope and appeal of pension mortgages have been widened by the rapid increase in the numbers of self-employed people making their own pension provisions, and from 1 July 1988 a change in the Inland Revenue rules allow individuals joining a personal portable pension scheme to retire and take a lump sum pension as early as age 50. For example, borrowers can take out a 25-year pension-linked mortgage at the age of 25, use the tax-free lump sum to pay off the mortgage and take a pension as soon as the policy matures (without actually retiring if they don't want to).

Pension mortgages do not always have to be repaid on retirement, however; many building societies will allow borrowers to continue to pay interest only on a mortgage if they wish to extend the loan.

Further changes in pension laws, allowing individuals to opt out of occupational pension schemes and take out their own personal portable pension schemes, removed the disincentive to change jobs, as intended; intentionally or not, it also created incentives for employees to opt out of the company scheme in order to join a portable pension scheme and use it for mortgage purposes. They could then take out a pension mortgage and so qualify for tax relief on the pension contribution element as well as the usual relief on interest on the mortgage.

A number of big company pension schemes and pension fund managers running occupational pension schemes have begun to offer pension mortgages for their members. Others may follow suit. If a company already offers pensions based on 'money-purchase' schemes – where benefits are based on the value of the investments made with the contributions – it is necessary to estimate the possible tax-free cash at retirement available to repay the mortgage. But most company schemes base the pension on the employee's salary in the final few years before retirement, and that salary is difficult to forecast 25 years in advance – which makes it difficult to judge how big a mortgage the pension scheme can support. So estimates are again required. It also remains to be seen what would happen to a company pension mortgage if the borrower wanted to change jobs or was made redundant. It could mean the heavy burden of paying off the mortgage over a short period or selling the house.

Pension mortgages accounted for less than 3 per cent of the mortgages arranged in 1986, but business began to grow rapidly in 1987. There were already more than 60 different lenders offering pension mortgages as an option, and banks and building societies, mortgage brokers and financial advisers had begun preparing a whole new range of pension mortgage products in anticipation of a further boom in business from portable pension schemes from July 1988.

The opportunity to take a tax-free lump sum on retirement is a crucial element of a pension mortgage. In the 1986 Budget, the Chancellor imposed a maximum limit of £150,000 on the size of tax-free lump sums paid on policies taken out from that date. That effectively means the most anyone can now borrow when taking on a pension mortgage policy is £150,000. The right to receive a lump sum free of tax on retirement has however always been an anomaly, and attracts regular criticism from a number of tax experts who say they are unfair to employees whose pensions do not permit lump-sum payments.

After the 1987 general election, the Chancellor of the Exchequer came under pressure to remove or reduce the tax exemption, making the lump sums liable to tax and reducing the capital sum that pension mortgages can make available to repay mortgage loans. But lump-sum payments are extremely popular with employees who qualify for them, especially in the Civil Service. The operators of pension mortgage schemes believe that the ceiling on the size of a tax-free lump sum, like the ceiling on mortgage interest tax relief, does at least mean that the concession will continue.

Mixed mortgages

Buyers may mix one or more types of mortgages on a single property. For example, borrowers who bought a house with an endowment mortgage may decide to take out a repayment mortgage to cover the extra money they may need when they move to a more expensive house, rather than take out another endowment policy – especially if they are elderly or in poor health and the premiums on a new endowment policy are very high. Borrowers with a pension mortgage may need an additional repayment mortgage if the guaranteed lump sum on their pension plan is not enough to cover the full amount they want to borrow.

7
Low-start mortgages

The steady rise in property prices in the mid-1980s made it increasingly difficult for first-time buyers to get a foot on the housing ladder, and in London and south-east England even yuppies and high-flyers earning big salaries and bigger commissions could not afford the mortgages they needed.

But the housing finance business was equal to the challenge, and produced a variety of low-start mortgages which cost substantially less than even a low-cost endowment mortgage, at least in the early years when borrowers normally find the burden of a mortgage heaviest. Low-start mortgages allow borrowers to take on a bigger mortgage than they could otherwise have done and to climb the housing ladder more quickly. Of course, 'low-start' implies 'high-finish' and the cost of a low-start mortgage eventually catches up and overtakes the cost of a 'regular' mortgage. But the first-time buyers hope by then to have found their feet, and the upwardly mobile professionals expect their incomes to have risen.

If incomes fail to match expectations, low-start mortgages can lead to problems, especially if property prices also fail to rise and houses turn out to be a disappointing investment. But that was unthinkable in the mid-1980s.

Low-start repayments

Most banks and some building societies still offer gross profile repayment mortgages, for which monthly payments in the early years can be 5–6 per cent lower than the payments on the net profile mortgages which are now more common.

Low-start endowments

Endowment policies can be adapted to produce reductions in the payment burden in the early years. Insurance companies achieve this by reducing the monthly premium borrowers pay in the early years and increasing it in the later years. A proportion of the monthly premium is still used to provide basic life insurance cover in case the borrower dies. But the contribution to the policy which eventually pays off the mortgage is cut back for the first few years, and increased later when the borrower can afford it. Since the endowment element of a low-cost mortgage accounts for about a fifth of the monthly payment, reducing the premiums by a third can cut the net monthly cost by roughly 6 per cent.

Norwich Union's Low-Start Endowment Plan, for example, starts off charging a single man, aged 30 and borrowing £30,000, a monthly premium of £22.20 a month, rising by 20 per cent a year until it reaches £44.40 a month in the sixth year. A normal policy premium would start and finish at a steady £38.40 a month, so the low-start borrower saves £16.20 a month and a total of £194.40 in the first year, and £457.92 in the first four years combined; but in the remaining years the low-start endowment will cost £1,458.72 more than a conventional policy. The interest charge – about £205.30 a month net at 11.25 per cent gross – is unaffected, so the total monthly payment in the first year is £226.80 a month.

Another variation marketed by the Halifax building society uses part of the mortgage loan to subsidize the monthly payments for a maximum of three years. At the end of that time the mortgage loan outstanding is higher than at the start. A low-start unit-linked mortgage scheme is available from an independent financial service company, CCL Financial Group.

Deferred-interest mortgages

Deferred-interest schemes produce much bigger savings in the early years than schemes based on reduced insurance premiums. The first deferred-interest scheme was devised by Royal Heritage in 1983, and a number of lenders, especially

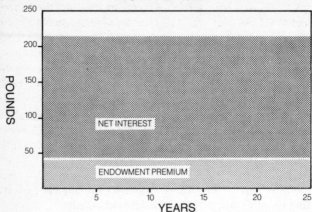

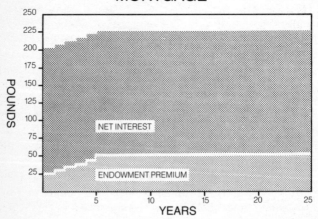

£30,000 mortgage over 25 years at 10% gross interest

These figures are based on a male aged 29

Figure 11
Low-start premiums start out lower than conventional ones, but end up higher; interest payments are unchanged.

foreign banks, some of the specialized mortgage lenders, such as City & Provincial, and one or two building societies have adopted them. The lenders agree to reduce the interest collected at first to as little as 70 per cent of the correct rate, say 7 per cent gross instead of 10 per cent. The rate will increase either in small annual steps or stay low for as long as five years. The unpaid interest is then added to the total amount borrowed, and the interest payments jump to the full rate on the increased amount. In the early years, deferred-interest schemes can reduce the monthly payments by as much as 30 per cent and allow borrowers to take on a bigger mortgage loan than they would otherwise have been able to afford. City & Provincial later took the process a stage further: in 1987 they introduced their Zero 12 policy, which gave borrowers a rebate of the full gross interest due on the mortgage for the first year, adding it to the capital amount to be paid back.

All deferred-interest schemes contain an element of 'live now, pay later'. The savings are real and here and now, but the total cost inevitably rises as the deferred interest builds up and starts to incur interest charges itself. The Inland Revenue will not allow tax relief on deferred interest. Deferred interest schemes are not available on repayment mortgages.

Low-start mortgages have proved very attractive to new lenders trying to carve out a share of the lending business at the expense of traditional lenders like building societies. They appeal to young professional people such as accountants and doctors, who earn relatively little in their early twenties but expect to earn much more in later life. And they appeal to anyone anxious to buy a more expensive house than they could afford with an ordinary mortgage.

Low-start mortgages allow them to take on much bigger mortgages than a conventional mortgage would allow – perhaps four times their annual income instead of only three times. Unlike a conventional mortgage, a low-start mortgage will inevitably go up in cost even if interest rates stay the same. But by then the young professional should be substantially higher up the earnings ladder, and well able to afford the extra cost of the later payments.

Mortgage brokers favour low-start mortgages because they

allow brokers to offer 'special packages' which help to advertise their other services, and estate agents like them because they allow buyers to reach further up the housing ladder and pay higher prices for property than they could otherwise afford to pay.

In theory, borrowers can take out a low-start mortgage and when the payments start to rise remortgage to obtain another low-start. But ultimately the costs must catch up on the borrower.

Low-start schemes also assume that property prices will stay ahead of inflation and that borrowers' incomes will rise even quicker. If they do not, low-start borrowers could be in difficulty. Lenders recognize the risks as well, and insist that the loan is appreciably smaller than the value of the property so that if the borrower cannot afford the increased payments when the time comes, the property is almost sure to be worth enough to repay the lender. Some lenders will lend only 70 per cent of the property's value; others will lend as much as 85 per cent, but no one would consider offering a low start on a 100 per cent advance. That automatically rules out first-time buyers who have no capital.

Even so, not everyone qualifies for a deferred-interest loan. Some lenders market them as 'executive' mortgages, available only to high fliers who are almost certain to be earning substantially more money and easily able to afford the increased payments when the interest jumps to the full rate. The Norwich & Peterborough building society's Executive Mortgage plan, for example, would lend up to four times the main borrower's income plus any second income, but would not advance more than 67 per cent of the value of the property.

Many variations on the theme have been developed. Regency Life Assurance, for example, introduced a low-start option which cuts monthly payments in the first year by as much as 30 per cent compared with a conventional repayment mortgage. Premiums then rise by 5 per cent a year until, between years 7 and 20, they are higher than a conventional mortgage; but payments then fall back to a lower rate for the last 5 years.

Flexible mortgages

Regency also offered a 'flexible option', which allows borrowers a certain amount of choice over what they pay and when they need the benefits of low payments, and when they can afford to shoulder the extra burdens. Interest rates usually start artificially low and rise later, but borrowers can choose to boost payments whenever they can afford it and then revert to lower payments. This alternative is designed to appeal mainly to the self-employed, who may have a run of good profits followed by years in which cash is short.

Bonus starts

Not every lender can afford to offer deferred-interest schemes. But a number of smaller lenders, including several of the small building societies, tempt borrowers with bonus schemes which offer new borrowers a small subsidy in the early years. Unlike low-start schemes, which offer substantially lower initial payments in return for higher payments later, bonus schemes are modest but free. The Melton Mowbray building society, the Clay Cross, the Sheffield, and the Newcastle all offered up to 0.5 per cent off the basic mortgage rate for a year. The Market Harborough offered a full one per cent off to borrowers who had saved with the society for six months, and the Vernon charged a lower rate for two years to borrowers who saved at least a 5 per cent deposit with the society and also agreed to accept the endowment policy chosen by the society. Bristol & West offered £200m of mortgages with 0.75 per cent off the interest rate in the first year as part of its 1988 'Winter Sale'. Some of the banks, led by Lloyds and Midland, have also now climbed on to the bandwagon – offering interest discounts to new borrowers for their first year.

Longer mortgages

One of the options sometimes available, especially to younger borrowers, is to take out a mortgage loan over a longer period. A £30,000 repayment mortgage which had to be paid off over

25 years at 10 per cent gross interest would cost £224.28 a month (after allowing for tax relief at the basic rate of 25p in the pound). The same mortgage over 30 years would cost £211.68 a month.

The total amount paid back over a longer period is much higher, of course. On the 25-year mortgage the 300 monthly repayments add up to £67,284, and over 30 years and 360 payments the borrower would pay back £76,205.

Some building societies will make loans for as long as 35 years, and the Halifax and the Walthamstow will go as far as 40 years for suitable applicants. To a basic rate taxpayer, the net cost of a £30,000 repayment mortgage at 10 per cent interest falls to £203.71 a month over 35 years and to £198.50 a month over 40 years, while the total amounts repaid escalate to £85,558 and £95,280 respectively.

Endowment mortgages offer a little less scope for savings, because no capital is being repaid, and the interest element is not affected by the length of the mortgage agreement. But monthly endowment premiums are lower over longer periods, because the insurance company has more time to build up the same maturity value. For a young borrower who could complete a 35- or 40-year endowment mortgage scheme by the time he or she reaches retirement age, the cost of a mortgage over a long period will still produce significant savings in monthly payments, although the total amount payable over a longer period escalates sharply.

Whether it is advisable to take on the much bigger total commitment will depend on what happens to house prices, interest rates and the level of inflation over the next 30 years or so. If interest rates remain well above the rate of inflation and house prices no longer continue to exceed inflation the answer will be no. But over the last 30 years longer loans have had the edge on shorter ones.

This is most clearly seen by comparing the choices open to a buyer who could afford a certain level of monthly payments. Anyone who bought a £2,500 house in 1956 and paid for it over 30 years would have been on much the same level of payments as someone who bought a house for £2,325 and paid for it over 25 years or a house for £2,080 and paid for it over 20 years, assuming an average interest rate of 6 per cent net. The total amount paid on the longest loan would have been around £5,450 compared with £3,600 on the shortest loan, but the more expensive house might now be worth £50,000 and the cheapest around £42,000.

Lenders have been reluctant to encourage borrowers to reduce initial payments by taking out mortgages over longer periods, partly to avoid tying up their own capital for longer periods, and have preferred to increase the multiples of income and the proportions of valuation they would be willing to lend. Insurance companies have also traditionally tailored their endowment insurance policies to 20- or 25-year terms to match lenders' requirements. Extending them to 35 or 40 years would substantially reduce the premiums and more borrowers would die before the policies mature. But it does seem likely that, if house prices continue to rise faster than earnings, lenders may be forced to consider longer mortgages – at least for young borrowers.

First-time buyers

The rise in property prices has put an increasing burden on first-time buyers, especially those who have little or no money saved up for a deposit and need a 95 per cent or 100 per cent mortgage. First-time buyers who have saved a modest deposit of £2,000–£3,000 are little better off. In the London area, where one-bedroom flats can cost over £40,000, first-time buyers need at least a £4,000 deposit to get a choice of lender.

With government approval, most building societies used to bias their lending policy to suit the first-time buyer, and charged a premium rate on bigger loans to better-off borrowers. But competition may well put a stop to most forms of favour. The banks have always been more pragmatic and have charged the same rates on large loans as on small ones. Only a handful of societies (including the National & Provincial and the Cardiff) continued to offer cheaper mortgages to first-time buyers at the end of 1987. A number of lenders are already charging lower rates on loans of £50,000 or more.

The time may not be far off when most lenders will offer

8
Interest rates

Until the last decade, borrowers had little or no choice of mortgage interest rate. Building society rates were set by the Building Societies Association at its monthly Council meeting. Rates on both mortgage loans and on investors' savings could be raised or lowered at a minimum of one month's notice, and all societies moved their rates at the same time and by the same amount. The BSA decided a basic rate – 11 per cent gross for mortgage loans and 8 per cent for savings, say – which would be the standard rate applied by all building societies.

All building societies charged higher rates on endowment mortgages and 'large' mortgages – loans for what the BSA regarded as abnormal amounts. A handful of smaller societies carved a niche for themselves by paying slightly higher rates to investors and charging more to borrowers wanting to buy unusual properties, including houses already partly occupied by sitting tenants, or shops with living accommodation above. But these special rates were still linked to the BSA rate.

The City of London building society offered borrowers a choice between the building society rate and a rate linked to the average yield on government War Loan stock. The link often produced a cheaper rate for borrowers, but it was a curiosity, introduced by City of London's then general manager, Anthony Trollope, and was quickly abandoned after his retirement.

The societies' cartel has now been abolished, and building societies now fix their own basic rates. But societies still calculate their interest charges in the same way, known as the 'annual rest' method. Using a formula they calculate the annual amount needed to pay the interest and capital on a repayment mortgage, and divide the result by 12 to arrive at the monthly repayment.

If interest rates rise or fall, the formula is used to recalculate the new payments needed to pay the loan off on time, and borrowers are notified of the change. Exactly how much the payments change depends on how much capital has already been repaid. Payments change rather less on a mortgage with only a few years left to maturity than on an identical loan in the early years, on which less capital has already been repaid. Capital repayments are also adjusted to reduce the effects of a change in interest rates. Inevitably this makes it difficult for individual borrowers to calculate the new level of payments for themselves.

Endowment and pension mortgages are much simpler to work out because the balance of the loan does not change at all during the life of the mortgage; the effect of a change in interest rates can be easily calculated and does not vary, regardless of how 'old' the mortgage is. Only the interest payments change, and the endowment or pension premiums remain unaffected by changes in interest rates.

The general level of interest rates on housing finance has risen appreciably in the last decade, partly because the government has used interest rates as the main means of controlling the demand for credit at home and of supporting sterling abroad. Increased competition has also had an effect on interest rates. Initially, at least, it seems to have pushed interest rates up because lenders have all been encouraged to bid up the cost of attracting the money they need to provide a plentiful supply of mortgage finance.

The entry of banks and specialized mortgage companies into the market has greatly increased the total level of competition in housing finance. Banks and other lenders set their own interest rates and make changes whenever they see a need or a commercial advantage; rates now change much more frequently. Greater competition also means that banks, building societies and other lenders are free to choose precisely how they calculate the payments due, as well as the basic level of interest they charge.

Lenders are all subject to the same commercial pressures and their interest rates do not in practice vary very much. It is rare to find differences as great as one per cent between the highest and lowest quoted mortgage rates on offer at any one time. But there are considerable differences in detail on the timing of changes, and the ways in which different lenders calculate interest. There are also some new ideas available, including fixed interest rates and index-linked rates.

Building society mortgage rates

All building societies can now choose the time when they alter interest rates, and so attempt to gain a competitive advantage. There are also minor variations in their standard rates; at any one time there could be differences as great as 0.5 per cent between the quoted rates different societies charge on standard mortgages. A number of smaller societies still charge premiums of up to one per cent on larger advances, but at least one charges less on larger loans. A handful still charge a higher rate for endowment mortgages, while one or two now charge more for repayment mortgages.

Bank mortgage rates

Banks get the money they need to provide mortgage loans from different sources. Some comes from customers' current accounts, on which banks usually pay no interest at all, some from deposit accounts on which the banks have to pay the income tax due before the investor receives the interest, and some from the London money markets, where the funds are usually cheaper because the interest is not taxed. The mix of money that banks receive is very different from that of the building societies, and mortgage lending also makes up only a part, usually about 15–20 per cent, of the banks' total lending business in sterling. That gives the banks opportunities to vary the size and timing of their mortgage rate changes to try to gain a commercial advantage over the building societies, which are still reluctant to change rates because of the very high costs of notifying customers.

The clearing banks tend to keep their mortgage loan rates between 1.5 per cent and 2 per cent above the base lending rates on which overdraft charges are calculated. The relationship is not fixed, and the mortgage rate is also affected by competition and by the banks' desire to increase or decrease their share of the mortgage market. But they are subject to the same sort of competitive pressures as the societies, and they cannot afford to keep rates fixed for long.

Mortgage companies and foreign banks get most of their money through long-term loans so they can afford to change rates less often, but even they will not fly in the face of market forces. They set their own rates, most of which are variable.

Market-linked rates

In a few cases mortgage lending rates are based directly on the cost of borrowing money in the London money market. Two American banks, Citibank and Chemical Bank, offer borrowers loans with the rate of interest 1 or 1.5 per cent above LIBOR (London Inter Bank Offered Rate), which is simply the average rate at which banks offer to lend each other money for a three-month period. Their mortgage rates are revised automatically every three months, based on the average market rate over the period since the last revision.

Index-linked rates

When the Treasury introduced index-linked government stocks, whose value rises in line with inflation, a number of lenders tried to follow the lead and introduce index-linked loans. Part of the loan was treated in the ordinary way. On the other part the lender charged a special low rate of interest, but the amount of capital the borrower had to repay was increased in line with the retail price index. So the borrower with a £20,000 loan might pay the going rate of interest on £10,000 and only 4 per cent interest on the other £10,000; but if retail prices went up 5 per cent in a year the capital debt would increase by 5 per cent of £10,000 (that is, £500). Index-linking of mortgages has not, however, caught on.

Fixed interest rates

From time to time various lenders, especially British and foreign banks, offer mortgage loans at a fixed rate of interest for a set period of time, usually a year but sometimes as long as three or even five years. Fixed rates are set slightly below the current variable rate to attract borrowers. Accepting a fixed rate loan is something of a gamble. If other interest rates go up or remain unchanged, borrowers who have accepted a fixed rate will benefit; if market rates come down, fixed-rate borrowers will regret the decision.

True interest rates

The rate of interest that lenders quote is the rate which most home buyers focus on. But it is not the true cost of borrowing, for a number of reasons. Lenders all quote a basic rate, which decides how much interest is due. But the true cost of borrowing the money depends not only on the rate of interest, but also on the way the interest due is calculated, when the interest is assessed and when it is paid, and also on survey and legal fees and any other charges which may be made for arranging the mortgage package.

Lenders are allowed to calculate the way they levy interest in different ways. On repayment mortgages, for example, all the building societies except the Guardian plus some of the banks, including the National Westminster and the TSB, still calculate the annual interest payable on the balance of the loan outstanding at the beginning of the year and divide the total annual interest and capital due by 12 to obtain the monthly payment. But as each payment includes a repayment of capital the borrower is being charged interest in the later months on capital which has already been repaid. In the first few years of a mortgage, when almost all the payments consist of interest, the difference is very small; but in the final years, when capital is being repaid rapidly, it can be considerable.

Most banks and mortgage companies (and the Guardian building society) eliminate this difference by calculating the interest payable on a reducing balance every month, giving borrowers full credit for the capital they have repaid each month, so that there is no extra cost involved.

On endowment and pension mortgages, no capital is being paid off at all during the life of the mortgage, so this question of extra costs from paying interest on capital already repaid does not arise. But interest is still being charged each month, and the Consumer Credit Act now requires all lenders to calculate the notional cost of paying interest monthly right from the start of a mortgage, to make sure that borrowers are aware of it.

The effects once again depend on when the interest is calculated and when it is actually paid. While most building societies, National Westminster and the TSB calculate interest on an annual balance and require it to be paid monthly, some banks including Barclays, Midland, Bank of Scotland and the Royal Bank of Scotland debit interest every three months, which makes the true cost of their endowment and pension mortgages slightly lower than that of building society mortgages on the same basic interest rate.

To complicate matters still more, Lloyds bank and the Guardian building society, although they calculate repayment mortgages on a reducing balance like the majority of the banks, debit interest every month, which makes the true cost slightly higher than that of the banks which debit quarterly. The effects are summarized in Table 14.

Even that is not quite the end of the story. The Consumer Credit Act also requires lenders to calculate the effect of fees on the cost of a mortgage. Lenders all insist that borrowers pay the cost of having a valuer inspect the property and the lender's legal fees in drawing up the mortgage agreement. Some lenders, but not all, also charge an arrangement fee. In some cases the costs can be added to the loan and paid off in instalments over the first 12 months. In most cases they have to be paid as soon as the mortgage has been arranged. But the Consumer Credit Act insists that fees also have to be taken into account as if they were averaged over the life of the mortgage. Exactly how much more they add to the cost of a mortgage depends on the fees, and they will vary from one house to another as well as one lender to another. For that reason they have been excluded from Table 14, but every lender has to calculate a current average and make it available to borrowers.

Annual percentage rates

Every lender has to publish the true cost of a typical mortgage loan – including the effects of capital repayments, the timing of interest charges and payments, and the effects of extra charges – in the form of an annual percentage rate (APR). Table 14 shows that the extra costs depend on the current rate of interest as well as the way they are calculated and paid. When basic interest rates are around 10 per cent, the timing of interest changes can add 0.3 or 0.4 per cent to the notional cost of endowment mortgages and pension mortgages, and 0.6 per cent to the cost of repayment mortgages from most building societies, National Westminster and the TSB.

If interest rates rise to 15 per cent, the additional cost will rise to about 0.8 per cent to 1.0 per cent on endowment and pension mortgages, and about 1.3 per cent on repayment mortgages from most building societies, National Westminster and the TSB. On top of that, the estimated cost of fees that lenders must include in their APRs will add about another 0.2 per cent to APRs in the table. APRs, by the way, must always be shown gross, excluding the effects of income tax relief.

Lenders are also obliged to tell borrowers the Total Amount

Table 14
Quoted and actual interest rates

Quoted rate (%)	Most societies, NatWest & TSB APR (%)		Barclays, Midland, Royal Bank Scotland APR (%) Repay. & Endow.	Lloyds Bank, Guardian BS APR (%) Repay. & Endow.
	Repay.	Endow.		
10	10.6	10.4	10.3	10.4
10.5	11.2	11.0	10.9	11.0
11	11.7	11.5	11.4	11.5
11.5	12.3	12.1	12.0	12.1
12	12.9	12.6	12.5	12.6
12.5	13.4	13.2	13.1	13.2
13	14.0	13.8	13.6	13.8

Source Building Societies Association

Payable (TAP) from start to finish on a mortgage, assuming that interest rates are unchanged, including the total gross interest cost plus the capital repayments and charges on a repayment mortgage, or the total interest and charges (but not insurance premiums) on an endowment or pension mortgage.

9
Buying a home – and finding the money

There is no 'right way' to buy a home. But the majority of buyers nowadays – especially first-time buyers – do plan ahead; this means setting about saving for a deposit and establishing how much they can borrow (and therefore the price they can afford to pay) before they start looking for a home to buy.

When they know how much they can spend, well organized buyers then draw up a list of requirements – the number of bedrooms, the style and design of the home they would prefer, any special requirements such as a study, a garden or a garage, ease of access to work by road or rail, and to shops and leisure facilities, family and friends. They then seek out the area that fits their requirements and start looking for a home.

There is no harm in looking around to get a good idea of what is available, and how prices are moving, at the same time as setting up the necessary loan. But it certainly helps to save vital time if the buyer has checked out the possible sources of finance and has a mortgage lined up before looking seriously at particular houses or flats.

Sellers are in a hurry, too. Cash buyers who do not need a mortgage and can buy without waiting for the approval of a third party are in the best position to clinch a deal. But only one buyer in six has the cash to buy outright these days. Out of the other five, the buyer who has planned ahead and can proceed with the greatest confidence and speed has a definite advantage over impulse buyers who see the home they want and only then start arranging a mortgage.

The house buying process gets more streamlined all the

time, and there is no shortage now of advice from banks and building societies, mortgage brokers and estate agents, who are only too pleased to explain the steps involved to potential customers who walk through the door. In London the First Time Homebuyers Advisory Service provides advice on where to look for property – mainly to young people and foreigners. It also acts as a mortgage broker, advising on the mortgages available and also on how to borrow high multiples of earnings and obtain low-start mortgages. The service is a commercial organization and charges a £10 registration fee and a £50 administration fee for arranging a repayment mortgage; on endowment mortgages it gets a commission from the insurance company. There are also several specialized monthly magazines, including the *Mortgage Magazine* and *What Mortgage?*, devoted to demystifying the sequence of events.

Buying a house or a flat involves a number of steps, and most borrowers need the services of a number of professionals. They include a mortgage adviser. This is someone who can help by advising you how much you can borrow, the range of options open to you, and the best choices available, and also start putting a mortgage package together. They come in several guises.

• An estate agent who will help you raise the money to buy the house or flat which he is trying to sell to you. If he succeeds he can earn commission from the seller and also from the insurance company which provides an endowment, unit-linked scheme or pension plan to go with the loan. If you choose a repayment mortgage, however, he may want a fee from you, and it is worth asking about that right at the start. Some estate agents are independent advisers who will have a duty to advise you on which kind of mortgage and which companies' policies have a good track record and are likely to be best for you. Others are tied agents, who have become sales representatives for mortgage loans and/or the policies supplied by one particular insurance company. Always find out at an early stage whether you are dealing with an independent (who will be a member of FIMBRA, the Financial Intermediaries, Managers and Brokers Regulatory Association) or a tied agent.

• A mortgage broker who will do the same job, either for a fee if you choose a repayment mortgage or for a commission from the company which supplies the endowment, investment or pension plan. Some brokers will be independent (and members of FIMBRA), which gives them an obligation to determine the best policy for the client, but others may be tied agents. Once again, make sure you know who you are dealing with.

● Building societies and banks will provide you with advice and guidance and not just lend the money. Most of them will advise on the choice between a repayment, an endowment, a unit-linked and a pension mortgage and a choice of insurance companies to supply the policies, to go with the loan they hope to provide you with themselves. They too will earn a commission, but the rates are fairly standard and once again the majority are independent. But about 40 building societies, including the Abbey National and the Chelsea, have signed up to supply policies from only one insurance company, and the number seems likely to increase.

How much can you borrow?

Most of the adult population in Britain qualifies for a mortgage, and so does most of the property. The question is: how much? Traditionally, lenders looked at both the buyer and the property before deciding whether to lend, and if so how much. Assessment in the past was rather slow and long-winded, and lenders had to be satisfied on both counts before offering a mortgage.

Recently, competition has forced all lenders to speed up and streamline the process. Mortgage brokers John Charcol claim to make a decision in five days. Others may take a week or two. They now look mainly at the borrower to see how much he or she can afford to borrow, and in the majority of cases will specify how much they will lend – so the borrower knows what properties are affordable. Lenders still need to look at the property to be sure that it is good security for the loan they are offering, but if they have already assessed the borrower the process is much quicker.

Earnings multiples

Lenders look at the borrower, or the borrowers in the case of joint applicants for a mortgage, to decide whether he, she or they are a good risk and whether they can repay the amount of the loan out of current and future income. The maximum loan an individual can get is a multiple of the borrower's annual income, usually 2.5 to 3 times, but these figures are subject to change according to circumstances. Self-employed people are normally expected to submit audited accounts for the previous three years to demonstrate how much they earn.

Other regular income can also be taken into consideration, although lenders will want to apply a lower multiple, and possibly no multiple at all, to overtime, commission bonuses or other earnings which are all considered less secure than a regular salary from full-time employment. So a borrower earning £10,000 a year could expect to borrow up to £30,000. With another £2,000 a year of regular overtime or commission income he or she could expect to borrow up to £32,000.

Joint incomes

At one time, lenders were reluctant to take the incomes of working wives into consideration in case they became pregnant and had to stop work. But family planning and pressure from the Equal Opportunities Commission have put a stop to discrimination, and all lenders are now obliged to take joint incomes into consideration. It is no longer just a question of principle. Rapidly rising property prices in the mid-1980s have made joint incomes increasingly important, both for young couples struggling to afford a home of their own, and for 'dinkie' couples (double income no kids), both in well paid jobs and anxious to borrow as much as possible to reach as far as they can up the housing ladder.

If borrowers are jointly buying a property but are not married, lenders until quite recently would have been reluctant to take a second income into consideration or even to lend at all. But that taboo has also now been swept away. The incomes of other partners, regardless of sex, are also taken into consideration exactly as if they were married.

According to the Nationwide Anglia building society about a

third of all new mortgage applications in 1987 were based on joint incomes. The proportion ranged from 25–30 per cent in Northern England to 44 per cent in London, where high house prices made it essential for many couples both to work in order to meet the higher mortgage payments.

In calculating a couple's loan ceiling, most lenders will still apply a lower multiple to the smaller of the two incomes, whether it is the man's or the woman's. Usually the lower income is simply added to the multiplied first income. So a couple earning £12,000 plus £8,000 could borrow say (£12,000 × 3) + £8,000 = £44,000. One or two lenders, for example the Derbyshire and the Sussex County building societies, might allow 1.5 times the second income.

Alternatively, an increasing number of lenders now give full value to both incomes, but apply a slightly lower lending multiple to the combined total. National Westminster, for example, has offered borrowers a choice of 3 times the main income plus the second income, or 2.5 times the combined incomes. This means that if a second borrower has an income more than one third of the first borrower's, they will get a bigger loan from a lender who gives both incomes equal treatment. For example if one borrower earns £15,000 and the other £6,000, the conventional formula will suggest a maximum loan of (3 × £15,000) + £6,000 = £51,000. The alternative will give 2.5 × (£15,000 + £6,000) = £52,500.

Some building societies, including the National & Provincial and the Guardian, also offer loans based on combined incomes, and some smaller societies, including the Leamington Spa, the Peckham and the Surrey, will lend 3 times joint income.

Some lenders will consider applications for equal weighting but are still reluctant to give full value to both incomes for young couples because of the higher risks that they may start a family, or split up. Some specify a minimum age of 25, and the Prudential, for example, will consider only couples who are both at least 30.

Existing debts

At one time, lenders applied another test, and limited the amount they would lend so that the borrower's net monthly payments would not exceed one week's income after tax; they also took into consideration other debt repayments including personal loans, hire purchase agreements and credit card repayments when deciding how much to lend. But most lenders now turn a blind eye to other debt repayments, on the assumption that they are mostly short-term debts which will be paid off within a matter of months.

Other factors

Income is by far the most important factor that lenders take into account in deciding the maximum they are willing to lend, and most lenders now claim that it is the only factor; but a few lenders still take the borrower's age and prospects into consideration. They might lend only 2.5 or 2.75 times the annual income to a middle-aged borrower who will retire well before the mortgage is paid off. Some lenders still prefer to see the bulk of the mortgage paid off by the time the borrower retires, and may require older borrowers – who will still be paying off a mortgage after retirement – to show that they will have a pension adequate to keep up the payments, allowing for the effects of inflation between now and then. Alternatively, lenders may reduce the proportion of the purchase price they are willing to lend to a borrower over 50 – from, say, 75 per cent of the property value to 60 per cent.

Higher multiples

At the other end of the scale, some lenders were willing to lend more than 3 times the annual income to borrowers with excellent prospects. At the height of the boom on the stock exchange in 1986–87, for example, some building societies and mortgage brokers were allowing yuppie couples earning high salaries in the City to borrow up to 4 times their income. Some lenders will advance up to 4 times annual income to borrowers with 'professional qualifications'. But multiples above 3 times the annual income are normally available only to borrowers who take out a low-start endowment mortgage, which reduces monthly payments in the early years of the mortgage by as much as 30 per cent below normal. The monthly payments on a low-start loan of 4 times the borrower's income are at first no higher than on a conventional loan of 3 times the income, although they will rise sharply in due course. Low-start mortgages are usually available only up to 65–75 per cent of the property value, which makes them suitable for borrowers with capital of their own to invest but not for borrowers who have little or no capital of their own. (See Chapter 7.)

High equity, non-status loans

How much an individual can borrow may also depend on what proportion of the total value of the property is involved. Anyone looking for a loan of 95 per cent or 100 per cent of the value of the property might be limited to, say, 2.75 times the main income, plus a second income. But for someone wanting to borrow between 75 per cent and 95 per cent of the value, the multiple might rise to 3 times the main income. On loans between 50 per cent and 75 per cent of the value, the multiple could rise to 3.25 times the income and anyone wanting to borrow less than 50 per cent of the value could expect to get up to 3.5 times his or her main income, plus a second income.

Some lenders, including The Mortgage Corporation and the National Home Loans Corporation, offer 'high equity' mortgages to borrowers who already have money of their own to invest and who are seeking a loan substantially less than the value of the property. The house itself is the main security if the borrower fails to make the payments, and the borrower's ability to repay out of earnings is less crucial.

Borrowers who are prepared to invest a sizeable amount of their own money also need to give less evidence of their income. When property prices were rising rapidly many lenders offered 'non-status' loans – they did not ask for bank references if borrowers wanted to borrow less than 70 per cent of the property's value. This was particularly useful for borrowers with erratic incomes and for the self-employed, but not much use to first-time buyers with little or no capital.

Future trends

Lending criteria are not fixed for all time. They depend on how easy it is to get credit, on the level of interest rates, the behaviour of property prices and on the level of confidence in the economy as a whole. When house prices show signs of levelling off, all lenders become rather more nervous about lending the full value of the property, in case borrowers get into financial difficulties or house prices begin to fall, leaving the borrower owing more than the house is worth and the mortgage not fully secured if the lender has to repossess it. The supply of 100 per cent mortgages, in particular, begins to dry up rapidly.

Lenders also have to be increasingly flexible. Rules are clearly no longer hard-and-fast, but depend on conditions and on the competition. Most lenders are willing to lend borrowers a higher multiple of their income, or to take more notice of bonuses and second incomes, when interest rates are low or falling and borrowers can expect the cost of the mortgage to come down. They discreetly reduce the multiple when interest rates are high and rising, in order to avoid the risk of borrowers taking on too big a burden and getting into financial difficulties. But if tax rates fall, lenders are often prepared to lend a higher multiple – especially to higher rate taxpayers, whose incomes after tax have risen. Anyone seriously thinking of buying property should always test the water by asking a lender or a broker for an up-to-date report on how much they would lend.

Mortgage guarantees

For the majority of borrowers, a quick decision is more important than the maximum loan. Borrowers these days have a far greater choice of lender than they did once. If a building society says no, a bank may say yes and vice versa. Under pressure of competition, more and more lenders – banks, building societies and mortgage companies alike – are now willing to assess the borrower's financial situation and give him or her a written guarantee of the maximum mortgage he or she can get.

The idea was pioneered by the Coventry building society which introduced a Mortgage Certificate, specifying how much the borrower could borrow on a suitable property, in June 1985. Other lenders were quick to follow with their own versions, including Abbey National's House to Home Mortgage Plan with a Mortgage Reservation Certificate which guarantees a mortgage of up to 70 per cent of the value of a suitable house without calling for a bank guarantee. Broker John Charcol took the process a step further with a Mortgage Guarantee Card which was not restricted to one lender.

Most of these guarantees are valid for three to six months. The assessment and the guarantee allow the borrower to go out and look for a property with the certain knowledge that if it is within his or her price range there will be no problem in raising the finance. The borrower can make decisions and act quickly, especially at times when property is selling fast and the first buyer with the money on the table wins the race.

A mortgage guarantee does not turn a borrower into a cash buyer, but the certificates are widely regarded as a statement of intent showing the holder is a serious buyer and not just a compulsive viewer of other people's houses. Lenders like to give them because even if borrowers fail to secure the property they want, the promise of a mortgage is likely to mean that they go back to the bank or building society which offered the guarantee, even if they choose a property from a different estate agent and come under pressure to look for a different lender.

Mortgage guarantees also give borrowers an up-to-date idea of the current state of the market. Armed with the knowledge of how much money he or she can borrow, the prudent house buyer is in a position to find a home to buy. But even mortgage guarantees are not the whole story. Even if the borrower's income and status are adequate, lenders will still want to inspect the property the borrower wants to buy, and to have it valued before deciding if it is a suitable security for a mortgage loan and how much they are willing to lend on it.

Valuing the property

Even if the would-be buyer passes the earnings test with flying colours, the property itself must also be suitable. It is the property that forms the security for the loan: if anything should go wrong, the property must be worth enough to pay the lender back and cover his costs, and ideally still not leave the borrower destitute. If the buyer wants to pay more than the lender is willing to lend he or she will have to find the extra out of savings. For first-time buyers with only modest savings, and for existing home owners wanting a much bigger loan to move a long way up the housing ladder, the valuation can be just as important as the amount they can afford to borrow. The amount a lender will advance on a particular property depends on two things: the valuation of the property, as determined by a professional valuer; and the proportion of that valuation that the lender is willing to advance.

Most high-street banks and building societies have their own staff of surveyors to carry out surveys of the property that borrowers want to buy. Some may also use independent surveyors in areas where they do not have a regular staff or at times when there is more work than their own surveyors can cope with. Other lenders, including overseas banks and the specialized mortgage companies, always use independent surveyors to carry out valuations for them.

Valuation and price

Traditionally, the surveyor's valuation is based on what the property would fetch if it had to be resold in a hurry, and is therefore usually rather less than the price the would-be buyer is willing to pay. If the surveyor's valuation is a little below the price of the property it does not necessarily mean that the property is not a good investment. Nor does it mean that it does not qualify for a loan – simply that the lender is being cautious, especially if the property is old, in an awkward location, or not in perfect repair. Small differences are not normally important. But a big difference between valuation and price is a warning that something or somebody is wrong.

For buyers with little capital of their own, the difference between the sale price and the surveyor's valuation can be the difference between affording a house and not being able to, and discrepancies between the market price and the surveyor's valuation have caused much misunderstanding and conflict over the years. But lenders and valuers are less cautious than they used to be – competition has seen to that. In practice, valuers have become much more liberal, especially in parts of the country where prices are rising fast, and they will often agree that the purchase price is a fair value. Where the property market is slow-moving, there could still be a discrepancy between the purchase price and the valuation, and the lender will limit the offer of a mortgage to a percentage of the purchase price *or* the valuation price, whichever is the lower of the two.

Percentage advances

The valuation itself is only the basis for arriving at the size of a loan. The percentage of the valuation that the lender is prepared to advance is also important. A house being sold for £55,000, for example, might be valued by the lender at only £50,000; the advance might be limited to 95 per cent of that, which is £47,500 – leaving the buyer to find £7,500 elsewhere.

Until recently, the more traditional lenders, including the banks and building societies, took the age and condition of the property into consideration in deciding how much they were willing to lend. On brand-new homes at times when building costs and property prices were rising rapidly, they were normally willing to make the valuation equal to the purchase price and to advance 100 per cent of the valuation, which would therefore cover the purchase price of the property in full. On big old houses built before 1919, lenders would normally have been reluctant to lend more than 50–60 per cent of the valuation, which is usually less than the price.

But competition and rising house prices have forced a change of attitude to property as well as to borrowers. Building societies have largely dropped their traditional prejudice against flats, though most lenders are still reluctant to lend money for the purchase of freehold flats. If the need arises to have repairs done which should properly be the shared responsibility of several freeholders, problems can arise in getting everyone to carry their share of the burden. Building societies are naturally reluctant to risk getting involved in such problems. Leasehold property is more acceptable because a leaseholder's responsibility is shared and the terms are enforceable under the conditions of the lease.

Most lenders do insist that leasehold property should have at least 20 years of lease unexpired after the mortgage has been repaid, but here again some lenders are more flexible than others. Most lenders are still reluctant to lend on flats above shops, and on mixed residential and commercial property, but a few lenders such as the Mornington building society welcome such propositions.

Other forms of residential property – flats and houses, terraced homes, town houses, semis and detached homes – are nowadays all equally acceptable. Most lenders, and especially the newer entrants to the mortgage market, insist that the type and age of property is immaterial. It is the value which matters. If a house or flat is worth the money, most lenders these days will advance 90 per cent of its value, some 95 per cent, and some 100 per cent.

But the proportion of the valuation that individual lenders will advance does still sometimes vary with the sheer size of the loan and with the status of the borrower. For example, a lender might be willing to advance 100 per cent of the valuation figure on a property worth less than £50,000, 90 per cent on houses between £50,000 and £100,000, 80 per cent above £150,000 and 70 per cent on property worth over £250,000, where prices can fluctuate much more.

Most lenders will offer a higher percentage of valuation to first-time buyers than to existing home owners, but this is based on the assumption that first-time buyers are likely to buy a cheaper property, not because their credit is better. On the contrary, they are less secure than existing home owners who have made a profit on their previous home. In the past, banks and building societies (at the insistence of the Treasury and the Bank of England) have required existing home owners to reinvest virtually all the profits on the home they are selling and have reduced the percentage they will lend on the next home to make sure they do so. But the Treasury and the Bank of England dropped the requirement at the end of 1986. If the government continues to relax controls and credit remains easy to get, lenders who are competing for customers may well decide that existing home owners are better risks and offer to lend them higher percentages of the property's value in future.

A number of lenders already offer borrowers with 'profess-ional status' and good prospects 5–10 per cent more of the purchase price than those whose income and prospects are not quite so secure. A qualified accountant, for example, would normally have no difficulty borrowing 95 per cent of the value of a suitable property, where a builder or a mechanic might find difficulty getting 90 per cent. Barristers and politicians, teachers and journalists might have to argue their case to get a high percentage of the value.

Maximum and minimum loans

Some lenders have rules on maximum and minimum mort-gages they are willing to grant. Most building societies do not set a minimum size of loan, but some banks are sometimes reluctant to lend less than £15,000 because of the extra cost of handling a number of small loans rather than one big one, and some foreign banks will not consider anyone asking for less than £30,000. Some lenders limit 100 per cent advances to loans below £50,000 or so, and many lenders will not consider lending more than 90 per cent or 95 per cent of the property value in any circumstances.

Most lenders also scale down the percentage of the property value they offer, according to the sheer size of the mortgage. Most small building societies, especially outside southern England, are still reluctant to lend more than about £50,000 to £70,000. But if the security is good, the bigger building societies, the banks and the newer lenders will cheerfully consider lending £500,000 or more to help buy residential property.

Future trends

The rules which lenders apply both to borrowers and to property in deciding how much to lend are of course subject to change with economic conditions and the current trends in interest rates, earnings and house prices. Competition also plays an important part. Individual lenders have to balance commercial prudence against their desire to win more business and increase their market share.

At the height of the property boom in 1986–88, yuppie couples could borrow up to 4 times their current annual income or 90–95 per cent of the value of the property they wanted to buy, simply by choosing a lender looking to win new business and using one of the low-start or deferred-interest plans. First-time buyers were often able to borrow the full purchase price. But the high multiples and the 100 per cent mortgages are the most likely categories to be cut back whenever the market looks less buoyant.

The category of borrower most vulnerable to changes in the mood of the house finance business is those who want to borrow the full purchase price of their property. In 1985, one-third of all first-time buyers were able to borrow the full valuation of their property. The big building societies – Halifax and Abbey National, Nationwide Anglia and the Woolwich – and a fair sprinkling of smaller societies, plus the TSB (Scotland) and Bank of Ireland Mortgages, Prudential Home Loans and Cannon Assurance, have all advertised 100 per cent mortgages. But banks and mortgage companies are very reluctant to lend the full value of a property and there is no doubt that 100 per cent mortgages became harder to get in 1986 and 1987 as demand for mortgage loans increased.

Large loans and low-start mortgages which go beyond the normal limits could also become much harder to get. There are and always will be a number of borrowers for whom every pound is vital in deciding which home to buy and whether they can afford the asking price for the place they want, especially in places like London where property prices are expensive. But most lenders are well aware that both borrowers and lenders are taking a risk. If interest rates rise or property prices fall, or if the stock market begins to fall and profits and commission incomes decline, borrowers who borrow to the limit could be in difficulties.

Most borrowers in fact neither need nor want to stretch their credit to the limit. Only a minority – probably no more than one in three of all first-time buyers and perhaps one in five of existing owner-occupiers on the move – need to push their borrowing power to its limits. Even in the fevered property market of the mid-1980s, first-time buyers borrowed on average only about 2 times their annual income, and existing owners borrowed only about 1.9 times their annual income – well below the maximum that lenders were willing to grant.

Advances as a proportion of the value of the property were also still well below the theoretical limits. The average advance which building societies were making was about 85 per cent of the price of the house to first-time buyers and 60 per cent to existing owners, producing a weighted average of about 70 per cent. Banks rarely make 100 per cent loans but their average advances were unlikely to be very much lower.

10
Extra costs – and extra cash

Most borrowers should have little difficulty these days in finding a mortgage loan which will cover between 75 per cent and 95 per cent of the cost of buying a home. But this still leaves borrowers to find more money to pay for the balance of the purchase price and the extra costs involved in buying.

It is possible to get a 100 per cent mortgage, which provides the buyer with the full price of the house or flat. But they are not always easy to get, and it is not advisable to borrow to the hilt. Unless they are desperate, even first-time buyers should aim to save up a down payment, which should be at least 5 per cent and preferably 10 per cent of the purchase price. The bigger their own investment is, the bigger choice of home they can buy (including older homes or converted flats) and the wider the choice of lender. Ideally, they ought also to have something in reserve to cope with emergencies as well.

House-buying expenses

Sellers of property pay the estate agent's fees, but the other costs and fees the buyer has to meet. These can add 3–5 per cent to the cost of buying a home.

Valuation and survey fees By law, property needs to be inspected by a surveyor to prepare a written valuation which decides how much the lender will offer to lend. Borrowers are still expected to pay the surveyors' fees, which work out between £50 and £100 on average. Almost all lenders nowadays let the buyer see the report. But the valuer's report is intended only to establish the current value of the property so far as the lender is concerned. It is not intended to check for faults which may need expensive repairs and it is not a guarantee that the property is in good condition. If the property is more than ten years old and not covered by a builder's guarantee, it is wise for the borrower also to pay for a structural survey to make sure there is no obvious fault in the property easily visible to a professional eye. A structural survey should be more detailed than the lender's valuation survey, but the same surveyor can carry out both surveys. Assuming he does so, the cost will usually be between £200 and £300, depending on the size of the property and its age.

Arrangement fees Most banks charge borrowers a fee for arranging a mortgage loan, which could be around £100. Prudential Home Loans charges £120 to £150 and The Mortgage Corporation charges £195. Most mortgage brokers will arrange endowment or pension mortgages free of charge and take their commission from the insurance company which supplies the policy. But they usually charge a fee of around 0.5 per cent of the value of the loan for arranging a repayment mortgage, on which they get no commission.

Stamp duty The government still levies a one per cent stamp duty on the full purchase price of all property costing over £30,000. Below that level there is no stamp duty to pay.

Land registry fees In many parts of the country it is obligatory still to pay fees to have the change of ownership registered with the Land Registry. The minimum fee is £20 on property worth up to £15,000, rising to £100 on property worth between £60,000 and £70,000 and £250 on property worth between £200,000 and £300,000.

Legal fees The buyer will also have to pay the cost of conveyancing – the legal process of transferring ownership, which has traditionally been done by a solicitor. Solicitors have finally been forced to give up their monopoly of conveyancing duties, and to allow competition from outsiders. A solicitor or licensed conveyancer employed by the buyer to carry out the conveyancing should also negotiate any special conditions, carry out searches to make sure the buyer has proper title, look out for covenants or development plans, and handle the payment of stamp duty and land registry fees. There are no fixed fees, but competition has reduced conveyancing charges from around £500 to as little as £150, and many reputable firms of solicitors will give written quotations on request. A few lenders and many brokers offer a free or cut-price package.

Although it is now perfectly possible for individuals to do their own conveyancing, searches and so on, lenders still insist on employing a solicitor or licensed conveyancer to handle their own side of the bargain – including drawing up the actual mortgage deed and transferring the money to the vendor's solicitors. The borrower is responsible for paying the lender's legal fees as well as his or her own. Most building societies will use the borrower's own solicitor, which cuts the cost to about £100 or so. But banks sometimes insist on using their own solicitors, costing as much as £250.

Competition has cut the cost of most of these items of expense, and according to a survey by the Woolwich building society the average buyer's costs came down from 3.2 per cent of the cost of the property in 1986 to 2.8 per cent in 1987. Firms such as Property Packs Ltd will provide a comprehensive service including conveyancing, legal costs and a valuation survey for £300 on a £30,000 house and £600 on a property costing £100,000.

Removal costs

The costs of physically moving can also add hundreds of pounds especially if a lot of furniture has to be packed, stored, moved and installed, or if new furniture or household goods have to be bought. Connection charges may also have to be paid to link up the gas, electricity, water and telephone, and there are rates to pay and travel costs to consider. Most buyers find some re-decoration and renovation is called for, however well maintained the property they are moving to.

Insurance

Borrowers who want to borrow more than 75–80 per cent of the value of a property (the precise proportion varies from one lender to another) usually have to take out a mortgage indemnity policy, so that if the borrower defaults on the loan the lender has a margin of protection against loss on repossessing and reselling the house. The cost of indemnity insurance rose steeply in 1986 and 1987 from as little as £2.50 per £1,000 to as much as £7 per £1,000 on amounts borrowed in excess of 75 per cent of the value of the property.

If a property is valued at £50,000, for example, the lender will usually insist on a mortgage indemnity policy to cover any loan over £37,500. A buyer needing to borrow £47,500 to buy the property would have to take out an indemnity policy to cover the £10,000 excess, and pay a premium of anything from £50 to £70.

Most lenders require the premium to be paid as a lump sum. Others will add the cost of the indemnity policy to the mortgage, and allow borrowers to pay it in monthly instalments over the first year, charging interest at one per cent above the ordinary mortgage rate but qualifying it for tax relief.

Buyers who borrow less than 75 per cent or so (the precise proportion depending on the lender's rules) do not need a mortgage indemnity policy. But borrowers who take out a repayment mortgage ought to have some basic life insurance which will provide enough to pay off the mortgage if the borrower dies before the loan is repaid. Some lenders insist that borrowers have enough life insurance before they will issue a repayment mortgage loan. Others merely point out that it is advisable, especially for a buyer with a family – so that they do not have to sell the house if the borrower dies. A plain life policy without profits, which would pay out £30,000 if the borrower dies within 25 years, might cost a healthy man of 30 about £100 a year. A policy which guarantees to pay out only the amount of the mortgage loan still owing at the time of death would be cheaper. Premiums for such a policy range from about £6 a month for a man of 60 to £4 a month for a man of 40 borrowing £30,000 over 25 years. Independent advisers will offer a choice of insurers, tied representatives will not.

Endowment mortgages incorporate life assurance as do most pension mortgage schemes.

Payment protection policies More and more lenders also

advise borrowers to take out income protection insurance to maintain mortgage payments if they are unable to work as a result of injury or illness, and insurance is also now available to cover the effects of redundancy. Staffordshire building society, for example, offers a Payment Protection Plan which will pay the mortgage for up to 18 months if the borrower becomes unemployed or cannot work because of an accident or illness. Some lenders offer built-in protection, for example Canada Life's unit-linked Homemaker Plan, which suspends premiums if the borrower becomes redundant or gets pregnant.

Buildings insurance Lenders also insist that borrowers take out insurance for the property, so that if the property is damaged or destroyed by fire, subsidence or some other accident, the borrower will receive enough compensation to repay the mortgage outstanding. Most lenders insist on the property insurance being enough to cover the replacement value of the property if it is destroyed, plus the incidental costs of housing the borrower and his or her family while the work is being done.

Lenders often insist on including the value of the land itself in deciding the amount of insurance they require the borrower to take out. Some borrowers may find they are being pressed to over-insure. But the responsibility for under-insurance – if the cost of rebuilding the property has risen to exceed the sum insured – remains the borrower's.

Traditionally lenders used to insist on having the property insured through a named insurance company. Most lenders now agree to accept insurance policies issued by any of the recognized insurance companies, although they may insist on a small fee, or waiver, to cover the commission they will lose.

Deposit

Buyers are expected to pay a deposit, usually 5–10 per cent of the purchase price, as soon as contracts have been exchanged. The deposit is part of the purchase price, but it usually has to be paid before the sale is absolutely final and the mortgage loan is paid over, and buyers may have to borrow the deposit from a friendly bank.

Bridging loans

Many first-time buyers have difficulty in finding the cash to make the down payment and to pay the expenses involved in buying a home before prices have risen and taken it out of reach again. Existing home owners usually have made some profit on the home they are selling; but they face instead the equally difficult problem of completing the purchase of a new home and paying a deposit at the same time as completing the sale and getting the money for the existing home. Almost inevitably there will be a delay of at least a few weeks.

Until the money from the original home comes in, a bridging loan is often the best way to pay the deposit on the second property and to pay the balance of the purchase price not covered by the mortgage loan. As well as mortgage tax relief borrowers can get additional tax relief on bridging loans for up to a year to help them finance a move.

Bridging loans are ideal when there is just a few weeks' delay between buying and selling. But many buyers at some stage or other find themselves in a 'chain' of sales, all of which are conditional on a buyer selling his or her own home to get the cash to pay for the house he or she wants to buy. If one buyer fails to sell, the whole chain of deals is held up. Buyers who are determined to move home often need additional cash to help them break the chain and complete the purchase of their next home before they have sold the previous one.

It is possible to keep two mortgages going for up to a year and claim tax relief on the interest paid on up to £30,000 of each loan. But financing two mortgages is still an expensive exercise, even if the lender providing the loan on the second property is willing to advance the mortgage before the first one has been paid off. Bridging loans are also an expensive way of going ahead with the purchase of one house before completing the sale of the other, especially if the buyer has to borrow the full purchase price and not just the capital tied up in the home for sale.

Bridging loans are more expensive than mortgage loans: most banks charge 3 per cent above their base lending rates. Banks used to have a virtual monopoly on bridging finance, and building societies were unable to help until the 1986 Act which also gave them the power to provide bridging loans. A handful of specialist companies such as Home Bridging have also moved into the market, offering to lend buyers enough to finance ownership of two properties for as long as it takes to sell the old home.

Chain breakers

A number of lenders have now produced packages which are alternatives to bridging loans. Prudential Property Services will buy outright the property a borrower needs to sell, in order to provide the cash to break a chain of waiting buyers. Several specialist firms, including Home Exchange and Home Equity Relocation, have been set up specifically to buy houses and break chains. Seekers, the 'property shop' group, will also break chains and many estate agents have for years been buying houses when a chain of sales and commissions are at stake.

But the price that chain breakers are willing to pay is usually 7.5–12.5 per cent below the market value, to cover the legal fees, stamp duty, selling costs, maintenance and insurance charges which the chain breaker incurs, as well as provide a margin of profit. And anyone who sells to a chain breaker may still fail to clinch the house he or she wants to buy, perhaps with the result of being out of the property market for a few weeks – a costly business if prices are rising strongly.

The Household Mortgage Corporation (HMC) offers another alternative: its 'Home Winner' scheme, available through estate agents. Home Winner charges interest initially only on the difference between the old and the new mortgage. For example, if a borrower has a mortgage for £30,000 on a house which remains unsold, and needs to take out a new mortgage for £50,000 to purchase a 'new' house, interest is initially charged on only £20,000. Interest on the other £30,000 borrowed is paid only when the original property is sold and the cash proceeds or existing policy become available. In the meantime, of course, the borrower has the benefit of any capital gain on the original property while waiting to sell it.

Supplementary finance

The additional costs involved in buying a house and moving home run into thousands of pounds. Until recently no mortgage lender was willing to take these costs into consideration. Competition has made all primary lenders more willing to consider lending enough to cover the additional costs associated with buying a house or moving, as well as the purchase itself. But if these lenders are not willing to go beyond a prudent figure limited by the resale value of the property or by the borrower's own earning power, mortgage brokers and other financial advisers may be able to put together packages of extra finance to help hard-pressed borrowers to cover the additional costs they will meet.

Some property developers tempt would-be buyers with offers of fully equipped kitchens or fully carpeted homes, and 100 per cent mortgages to cover the inclusive cost. But this can be a dangerous temptation to buyers who are stretched for cash, because the value of the fittings and furnishings is unlikely to be recovered if the property has to be resold quickly.

At every stage however there are some extra sources of cash worth considering. A friendly bank manager might well be willing to allow a valued customer an overdraft for a few months to meet the inevitable short-term expenses. It is worth asking. Failing an overdraft, banks (and, more recently, building societies) will often offer a personal loan, which carries a fixed rate of interest and is repaid in regular instalments over a period of up to three years. Most of the bigger societies are also able to offer personal loans up to £5,000.

Homeloan scheme

The government some years ago recognized the need to help first-time buyers to find a down payment, and introduced the Homeloan scheme. First-time buyers who are buying low-cost housing below a certain price level, which varies from one part of the country to another, can borrow up to £600 interest-free for five years if they have saved a similar sum themselves. They also qualify for a grant of £110. But the amount of the loan and grant has not been raised in line with rising costs and is no longer adequate to meet the true costs of trying to buy a home; in recent years only a few thousand borrowers have applied for a Homeloan scheme each year.

Top-up loans

Thousands of borrowers found themselves unable to borrow all the money they needed to buy their homes during the property price explosion in the early 1970s, and took out top-up loans – mainly from insurance companies who were often 'introduced' by the main lender. Insurance companies who supplied top-up loans were able to charge a higher rate of interest, often 2 per cent more than the cost of the mortgage loan itself, and also required the borrower to take out another insurance policy.

As building societies became more competitive and began to adjust to an era of rapidly rising property prices, the need for top-up mortgages diminished. But the surge in property prices in the mid-1980s created a fresh demand for top-up loans from a new generation of people desperate to borrow the absolute maximum, and created new opportunities for mortgage brokers and others to find extra cash for borrowers. About a dozen insurance companies have been willing to offer top-up loans, backed up by endowment policies or unit-linked investments including Commercial Union, Cornhill, Eagle Star, General Accident, Imperial, Norwich Union, Reliance Mutual, Royal Heritage, Scottish Amicable, Scottish Equitable, Scottish Mutual and Sun Alliance.

The qualifications for a top-up mortgage are similar to those for first mortgages. Most kinds of property and most people are eligible, and the maximum amount that can be borrowed is based on the borrower's income and the property's value – although lenders' rules tend to differ much more than first-mortgage lenders do. Some will go as high as 3.5 times income and 100 per cent of valuation, while others are more restrictive, and many put a limit on the top-up loan as a proportion of the first mortgage and/or as a cash sum. Norwich Union, for example, will match a first mortgage but only up to £50,000. Most lenders charge a slightly higher interest rate than on a first mortgage, and some specify the kind of policies they require borrowers to take, although only one or two may still insist on a without-profits endowment.

Second mortgages

Many borrowers over the years have raised extra cash using their already mortgaged property as security. A second mortgage is usually quite a separate transaction, although the first lender is always informed. The principal lender who holds the first mortgage has first claim on the assets in full and the second mortgagee runs the risk that there will not be enough left to pay back the loan if the property has to be sold.

Since a second mortgage must raise the percentage of debt outstanding on a property there is a distinct element of risk in a second mortgage, and interest rates are appreciably higher than on first mortgages. Borrowers who want a second mortgage on their property also have to pay for a new valuation survey, plus the legal costs, an administrative charge and probably another indemnity premium which will give the second lender some protection if the borrower fails to make the payments required.

The interest rates charged by finance houses, in particular, are high, because they tend to deal with customers they do not know and so face a high incidence of bad debt. Banks are usually willing to offer second mortgages at lower interest rates, especially to customers they know, but in most cases they require second mortgages to be repaid in five to seven years. Building societies were not allowed to make second mortgages until January 1987. Even now they would not normally do so, but the bigger societies can and do now offer personal loans which serve the same purpose.

Further advances

Borrowers who need to raise extra money are best advised to ask their original lender for a further advance first. The rapid rise in house prices over the years has encouraged many existing home owners to try to borrow more money, either to improve their property and further enhance its value through repairs and extensions, or simply to use their home as security to raise money for some totally different purpose, ranging from buying cars to investing in a business.

Further advances to finance home improvements have the great advantage that the interest rate charged and the repayment period are usually the same as those of the original mortgage. The interest also used to be tax deductible, but this concession was withdrawn in the 1988 Budget for further advances taken out from 6 April 1988. Lenders might want to inspect the property to make sure that the further advance is still covered by the value of the property. After years of rising prices, lenders normally waive the rule, but they will ask for a commitment fee, usually one per cent of the additional loan.

Until 1987, the only legitimate reason for getting a further advance was to help finance the building of extensions or the installation of home improvements. Raising extra money for home improvements became an important additional element in the housing finance market. Building societies used to insist that borrowers undertake repairs and improvements to a property within the first few months of buying it. Often they used to withhold a proportion of the mortgage until the work had been carried out to their satisfaction. Competition with the banks has in some cases eliminated this kind of problematic requirement. But many house buyers voluntarily decide to improve their home by installing a new kitchen or bathroom, rewiring or installing central heating, for example.

Table 15
New mortgages and further advances

Year	New mortgages		Further advances			
	Number (000)	Value (£m)	Number (000)	(%)	Value (£)	(%)
1970	528	1,888	79	13	42	2.2
1974	431	2,804	98	18	110	3.7
1978	820	8,251	344	29	516	5.9
1982	862	13,735	443	33	1,258	8.4
1986	1,333	32,864	698	34	2,908	8.1

The % columns express further advances as a proportion of total new loans.
Source Building Societies Association

Home improvement loans have not always been easy to get. Building societies have been happy to lend existing borrowers the money to pay for home improvements when demand for new mortgages was slack – finance for home improvements was a good way of lending surplus funds profitably and cheaply, without the need for further surveys and administrative expense. When demand for mortgages was strong, however, building societies again rationed the money available for home improvements.

The entry of the banks into the mortgage market forced the building societies to give home improvements a higher priority. In 1970, further advances made up only one in eight of the applications that building societies approved and only 2 per cent of the total amount they lent that year. But further advances rose to about 4 per cent of total building society lending by the mid-1970s, and grew rapidly after the banks re-entered the mortgage market in the early 1980s. By the middle of the decade, additional loans accounted for 30 per cent of all new mortgage advances and 7–8 per cent of the money building societies lent each year.

Some building societies have made a particular effort to build up their home improvement lending. Leading the field is the Sheffield, which lent over 20 per cent of its money for home improvements in 1987, followed by the Gainsborough, the Tipton & Coseley and the North of England. The demand for home improvement loans seems to be higher in the north where property values are rising less fast, and least in the south, where buyers tend to move on rather than stay and improve.

Further advances cover a wide range of expenditure from central heating and double glazing to major items such as a new roof or building an extension. On larger items of spending, many lenders are happy to add the extra loan to the existing mortgage and let it be repaid at the same rate of interest and over the same period as the original mortgage.

The sudden withdrawal of tax relief on the interest on home improvement loans with effect from 6 April 1988 may reduce demand quite sharply. But other types of lending will probably fill the gap.

Mortgage money for other uses

Although home improvements were the only legitimate excuse for obtaining tax relief on the interest on further advances, for years borrowers have been bending the rules and diverting some if not all the extra money to spend on anything from cars and consumer durables to foreign holidays or school fees. The sudden surge in demand for further advances began immediately after interest on other forms of borrowing was disallowed for tax relief in 1969. It seems only logical to assume that a substantial proportion of the money being lent as further advances in the past 15 to 20 years – perhaps as much as half – has been used for purposes which strictly speaking had nothing to do with housing, and many borrowers have still claimed tax relief on the interest.

Borrowers have also taken the opportunity to try to increase their mortgage borrowing when moving house, by asking for a higher percentage loan than they really need to buy the new property, and using the extra cash for other purposes. Some lenders have insisted on profits on the sale of the existing home being reinvested, but others have always been more obliging. The Bank of England and the Inland Revenue have watched the trend towards using mortgage money for other purposes for some years, and in January 1982 sent letters to all banks and building societies asking them to ensure that further advances to existing borrowers and the bigger mortgages given to home owners moving house were used strictly for housing, and not milked to provide cheap funds for other purposes. In 1986 the Bank of England rejected a plan by bankers Kleinwort Benson to lend money secured on property specifically to spend on other things.

But growing competition between different lenders has made it impractical to expect lenders to police all applications in detail, or to refuse to lend money in conditions where borrowers can quickly and easily take their business to another lender who may be less scrupulous. Competition multiplied the opportunities for borrowers to extract loans from the mortgage market for other purposes.

Remortgages

Thanks to the increased competition in the housing finance market, borrowers who already have a mortgage and are financially sound have found that they can borrow money quite easily by remortgaging their existing property with a different lender and paying off the original mortgage. Until recently, remortgage applications were not widely welcomed and most lenders who would consider a proposal charged a higher rate of interest. But remortgages have become increasingly acceptable to lenders, and only a handful of lenders, mostly small building societies, still charge a higher rate of interest on a remortgage.

Since 1980, when the banks began seriously competing with the building societies, the net amount of money being borrowed through the housing finance market has more than doubled, even after allowing for inflation. Thousands of home owners have been able quite successfully to pay off a mortgage and remortgage their home with another lender for a larger sum, ostensibly to take advantage of a lower rate of interest, but with the added attraction of being able to use the extra money to buy cars or boats, or pay for school fees or foreign holidays. Although the practice was and is illegal, it seems certain that many borrowers were also able to claim tax relief on the interest.

In December 1986 the Treasury and the Bank of England formally withdrew the instructions to banks and building societies to ensure that borrowers did not use mortgage money for purposes other than home buying and improvement. Government policy now recognizes the right of owners of residential property to use their own homes as security to borrow money for other purposes.

Within a year of the Bank of England's relaxing its rules, the National Home Loans Corporation estimated that up to 40 per cent of the loans it was granting were remortgages, where borrowers took out a new loan and paid off their original mortgage without any intention of moving home. Comprehensive figures are not yet available, but it is possible that as many as 10 per cent of all new mortgage loans in 1987 were remortgages, carried out either to take advantage of a slightly cheaper going rate of interest, or to extract some of the capital value out of the borrower's home to use for other purposes.

Borrowers who remortgage must expect to pay all the charges, including survey fees and legal fees, as if they were starting from scratch. The withdrawal of tax relief on home improvement loans means remortgages can really be justified only if they can take advantage of a cheaper interest rate – there will be no extra tax relief if the amount borrowed is increased. Applications may well fall sharply.

Home equity loans

The change in emphasis means, however, that lenders can now freely offer additional loans which are backed by the borrower's stake in his or her property (that is, the difference between the property's value and the amount of mortgage and other debts outstanding on the property). Home equity loans, as they are generally called, do not qualify for tax relief, and the rate of interest is often higher than on a mortgage loan and is fixed independently of mortgage rates. But because the loans are secured by property (and the risk of the lender being unable to recover his money if the borrower fails to pay is therefore much less), interest rates are generally lower than overdraft rates and much lower than on personal loans, credit cards or other forms of consumer credit. There is usually a small administrative charge, but it will be much less than the cost of a remortgage with a different lender.

National Westminster bank's home equity loans, introduced in January 1988, offered additional loans to existing mortgage customers from a minimum of £5,000 in units of £2,000 up to 80 per cent of the home owner's equity (the property value less the outstanding mortgage), over any period from five years up to the mortgage repayment date.

Another variation, pioneered by the Bank of Scotland in association with Sun Life of Canada, allows home owners to borrow up to 80 per cent of their property's value, minus any outstanding mortgage. The money does not have to be borrowed at once, and borrowers are given a cheque-book to draw whenever they want, paying interest of about 1 per cent above the mortgage rate, and only on money actually drawn. But the scheme is not available to borrowers who have retired. Home equity loans are expected to be increasingly popular, and are not limited to the lenders' existing customers.

11
Choosing a mortgage

Henry Ford is supposed to have said that his customers could have any colour of car they wanted, provided it was black. House buyers once faced a similar choice: there were a great many building societies, but the mortgages they offered were all the same. That situation has now gone for good. The modern borrower has a choice of well over 200 different lenders, all offering four or five different basic types of mortgage deal. The size of loan any borrower can obtain to buy the same property will vary by as much as 50 per cent according to the way different lenders calculate the amounts they are willing to advance. Even the rates of interest charged by different lenders vary by as much as one per cent.

Choosing a mortgage can now be almost as complicated as choosing a house. It is also a relatively long-term business. Just as it is impossible to guarantee which house or which district will turn out to be the best investment over a period of 10, 20 or 30 years, so it is impossible to say for sure which mortgage will be the Best Buy in the long term as well as the short.

Almost everyone now has a choice. First-time buyers are usually sure of a welcome if they are not being too ambitious in their choice of a first home. Although banks and building societies are much more commercial than they used to be, they still tend to have a soft spot for first-timers, who could become good customers for life. Many building societies will give first-time buyers 100 per cent mortgages if they are looking for loans below a certain figure. In most cases this is around £40,000 to £50,000, but the Halifax will give 100 per cent mortgages of up to £75,000.

Buyers with a home to sell, able to provide a substantial down payment, should also have no difficulty in finding any number of lenders willing to offer a mortgage – especially if the borrower has a good job with steady prospects, the loan is less than 2.5 times his or her annual income, and he or she is buying a new home put up by a reputable builder. Older borrowers can often find lenders willing to offer 'interest-only' loans, repayable only when the property is sold.

Older properties are no longer regarded with suspicion, and most lenders are much more concerned with the value of a property than its age. If a buyer wants to borrow up to 95 per cent of the current value of the home there will be little difficulty in persuading any bank or building society to lend, provided the other elements are right. Older borrowers with less secure jobs and prospects might find it harder to borrow heavily to buy very expensive property, but they should be able to borrow up to 75 per cent of the purchase price or 2.5 times their annual income.

Lenders are becoming more fashion-conscious as well as profit-conscious than they used to be. Yuppies with bright financial prospects will find lenders falling over themselves to offer them mortgages while the economy is expanding and everything is looking rosy. They can pick and choose. If the economy slows down, however, yuppies may find themselves out of favour, and lenders may positively prefer to lend to dependable stick-in-the-muds.

Which lender?

The great majority of borrowers can and do get what they want from the first lender they ask. That is why the banks and building societies still compete to open branches in the busiest high streets and in places where there are plenty of offices and shops to bring the public past their door. They know that most people will call in at the most convenient branch to home or office, especially if it is also the place where they have been keeping their savings. Estate agents are also ideally placed to pick up business when customers come in to look for somewhere to buy.

The days have gone, perhaps for ever, when it was essential to have a savings account with a building society for at least a year to have any chance of getting a mortgage, but the arrangement is convenient and helps to establish mutual confidence. As an alternative, more people now think of asking a bank for a mortgage. Usually borrowers go to the branch where they keep their account. But it is not absolutely necessary to have an account, or to open one.

Buyers who need to borrow virtually the whole of the purchase price may find life rather harder. Building societies are generally willing to consider 100 per cent mortgages, but only to first-time buyers wanting modest loans. If societies are periodically short of funds – for example, if their interest rates to savers are temporarily below competing rates offered by competitors, or if investors are withdrawing savings heavily in order to buy shares in a government privatization scheme – then the supply of 100 per cent mortgages can be severely limited. Banks and mortgage companies are more conservative. Most lend a maximum of 90 per cent or 95 per cent of the price or of their valuation of a property.

Relatively few people try a foreign bank, a finance house, an insurance company or a mortgage company, or seriously shop around a variety of sources of finance; but the proportion who do is rising rapidly, and more and more people now actively seek advice, by buying books, reading newspapers or asking for professional guidance. The new generation of lenders, including foreign banks and mortgage companies, get most of their business through financial advisers, estate agents, insurance brokers or mortgage brokers, and it is well worth shopping around these sources. Insurance companies also get an increasing proportion of their business by providing endowment policies, unit-linked investments and pension schemes. Some have their own sales force, others market their products through financial advisers, estate agents and brokers.

Anyone who is looking for something special – a very big mortgage on an unusual kind of property, say – may have to try a number of sources in order to find a lender. And even the ordinary borrower really ought to ask for a quotation from a bank, a building society and one or more of the other lenders.

The biggest loans

For some borrowers the most important single question is where and how to borrow the most money. They are known in the mortgage business as the 'maximizers', who want to borrow the most in order to get as far up the housing ladder as possible in one step, believing that a house is a guaranteed good investment and the more expensive it is the better. Whether a big mortgage is really in the borrower's best interests will depend on how well his or her income prospects turn out, whether property prices continue to rise faster than other prices, and on the level of mortgage interest rates.

In recent years, rising incomes have quickly reduced the burden of even the biggest mortgage, and rising house prices have helped big borrowers to make big, quick profits on their homes. Anyone who borrows £50,000 to buy a house for £60,000, for example, owns just £10,000 worth of bricks and mortar at the start. But if the house price rises by 50 per cent to £90,000, the borrower can sell it, pay back the mortgage and walk away with £40,000, which is four times the original investment.

But if house prices fall, as they did in the 1930s, and have done recently in parts of the United States, a borrower with a big mortgage can find that the mortgage debt is more than the property is now worth. Even if house prices rise, mortgage interest rates could increase steeply and borrowers with big mortgages could find the cost of monthly payments become an intolerable burden.

For anyone with a big enough income to pay for it, finding a big mortgage is no longer a problem. Most banks and the larger building societies will lend up to £500,000 or even more to the right customer for the right property. Borrowers who need to go beyond three times their income should look for a lender such as the Skipton or the Norwich & Peterborough building societies – the latter offers up to four times the borrower's income on its Professional and Executive Plan mortgages – or ask a mortgage broker to recommend a lender offering low-start mortgages.

A top-up mortgage may also be the answer for borrowers

with little capital of their own who also want to borrow a large multiple of their income. But for most people it is a question of finding who will lend up to three times the borrower's main annual income and take other sources of income into account, or will give the best multiple of combined incomes.

No one lender – bank, building society, insurance company or mortgage company – will offer the best deal in all circumstances, and there is no entirely reliable substitute for shopping around to see whose evaluation of an individual's or a couple's pattern of earnings is most favourable. The best alternative is to ask a broker to do the work and call the choices up on-screen, and then find out how much the competing packages cost.

In the last year or two, foreign banks and the new mortgage companies have often been the best sources of large loans. It suits them to be so because they can build up their market share more rapidly, or easily commit the money they wish to lend and keep their administrative costs to a minimum by concentrating their lending in a smaller number of large loans.

The cheapest money

The rate of interest lenders will charge also ranks high on most borrowers' list of priorities. But the differences between one lender and another are less marked in this respect. The most important decision a borrower may face is whether to go for a fixed-rate mortgage – if any are on offer at the time – or to opt for a conventional variable-interest rate, which the lender can change at a few weeks' notice.

Fixed-rate mortgages are still relatively hard to come by. In the days when inflation was running in double figures, no one would have taken the risk of either borrowing or lending at a fixed rate of interest and then finding rates moving the wrong way. It is less of a gamble when inflation and interest rates are relatively steady, but memories of double-figure inflation rates in the 1970s are still fresh.

The clearing banks occasionally do find that they can borrow an amount of money at a fixed rate which they can relend at a profit. But fixed-rate mortgages are generally available for only a limited time or until the lender has used up the money set aside for the purpose. Whenever they have been offered recently there has been a rush of borrowers and the banks have run out of fixed-rate cash very quickly.

Fixed-rate mortgages are always offered below the going rate on variable-rate mortgages; no one would rush to borrow if the fixed rate were higher. But they are not necessarily a bargain. Lenders offer fixed-rate loans only when they think there is a strong possibility that interest rates generally will be coming down. If interest rates in the economy stay unchanged or even rise, the borrower who has agreed to pay a fixed rate of interest keeps the advantage. If rates generally do come down, as the lenders expect them to, borrowers will find themselves committed to paying the fixed rate of interest while their neighbours with a variable-rate mortgage enjoy the benefit of lower payments.

When lenders think rates are going to rise, the supply of fixed rate mortgages dries up, and availability is therefore irregular as well as limited in amounts. Fixed-rate mortgages could become more important, but for the time being less than one per cent of the mortgages outstanding are fixed-rate and even they usually apply for only the first two or three years.

For the majority of borrowers the choice is between various kinds of floating-rate mortgages. The choice is now wider than ever, but the business is very competitive and the differences are generally modest. The cheapest rates in recent years have come from the mortgage companies and especially The Mortgage Corporation, as they exploit the advantages of having low operating costs and access to cheap money in the London money markets. Among insurance companies, Eagle Star has offered low interest rates to borrowers who choose a without-profits endowment mortgage, which pays no bonus to the borrower when it reaches maturity.

But rates are all subject to change at short notice, and only a handful of lenders actually promise to maintain an advantage over the rates the big building societies charge. Banks and building societies, insurance companies and mortgage companies all now fix their own mortgage rates independently, and at any one time one or the other may be the cheapest. They also calculate their interest rates differently, and the only reliable way to find the cheapest is to look for the Annual Percentage Rate (APR), however fine the print it is buried in.

In recent years, competition has encouraged lenders to offer bonus interest rates for new borrowers, usually 0.5 per cent off the normal rate for the first year. Bonuses are genuine incentives, which can save the average borrower around £100 to £150 after tax relief. But they are temporary reductions in the mortgage burden, and the rate soon reverts to normal – so a bonus is no substitute for a lower long-term rate. Low-start mortgages are also attractive to borrowers who need to borrow every penny they can now and keep the cost of the mortgage low in the first few years. But the costs go up when the low-start period ends.

Banks, building societies and everyone else who offers variable-rate mortgage loans are all free to change their rates in the future, usually with no more than a few weeks' notice. There is no cast-iron guarantee that whichever lender offers the lowest rate today will stay the cheapest in the future. As a rule of thumb, building societies still change their rates less often than the banks, so banks may steal an advantage by cutting rates first when the trend is downwards, but it could work the other way if rates are rising.

Banks are likely to be marginally cheaper whenever they are actively trying to increase their market share, but they rely much less than building societies on mortgage lending. They could decide they have all the business they need and let their rate become uncompetitive to choke off demand. Banks are also closer to the front line of government policy on credit. In recent years they have been relatively free to lend as much as they feel is commercially sound, but if in future they ever come under direct pressure to cut back the general level of lending there is a possibility they may have to raise mortgage rates in order to discourage new business and give a higher priority to commercial customers.

But banks do have the advantage that the bulk of the funds they need to finance their mortgage lending can be raised in the London money market. In recent years, bulk deposits in the money market, where banks borrow from and lend to each other, have been considerably cheaper than the cost of raising money from small investors, on whom building societies still rely for most of their money. Mortgage companies, which borrow all their money in the money market, have often been the cheapest lenders of all. Although they earn no commission on endowment mortgages (unlike building societies and banks), their overhead costs are lower because they have no salesmen or branch offices to pay for. The cost of the money they use has also been lower in recent years. But there is no guarantee this will always be the case.

What type of mortgage?

Well under half of those who have taken out a new mortgage since 1983 have chosen a repayment mortgage, and in 1987 the proportion choosing a repayment was down to about a quarter. The majority of new borrowers now choose from various forms of endowment or pension-linked mortgages, and the banks, building societies and other lenders have actively encouraged the trend by pointing out the attractions of a tax-free lump sum as well as having the mortgage paid off when the policy matures.

The case for repayment mortgages is now often neglected because they have no supporters with a vested interest in promoting them. The 'great debate' over the merits of repayment and endowment mortgages seems to have ended in favour of the endowment. The prospect of a tax-free bonus in addition to paying off the mortgage is a decisive argument for the majority of borrowers. But ignoring the bonus, because it is not guaranteed, there is still something to be said for both types.

Repayment mortgages were traditionally cheaper than endowments, but that is no longer always the case, now that higher interest rates on endowment mortgages have been abolished. To start with, there is little to choose between the annual payments on a repayment mortgage or a low-start endowment mortgage of the same size. But interest payments and therefore tax relief continue at a high level on an endowment mortgage, whereas they both diminish as capital is repaid on a repayment mortgage.

With tax relief, the endowment mortgage works out considerably cheaper for a basic-rate taxpayer over a 20-year period, the two are much the same over 25 years but a repayment mortgage could be the cheaper over 30 years (in terms of total payments, and ignoring any bonus paid by the endowment policy on maturity).

For higher-rate taxpayers, the advantages of an endowment are even greater. A borrower who is paying a substantial amount of tax at 40 per cent, for example, finds the endowment policy is cheaper over 20 and 25 years because of the continuing tax relief on the interest payments, and a repayment mortgage only becomes cheaper after 30 years or more. Once account is taken of the need for basic life insurance on a repayment mortgage and the prospect of a bonus when the endowment mortgage matures, the balance shifts even more in favour of an endowment.

Higher-rate taxpayers with repayment mortgages over £30,000 also start to lose some of the higher-rate tax relief as soon as the balance of capital owed drops below £30,000 – whereas basic-rate taxpayers making constant net repayments under MIRAS are not affected. Higher-rate taxpayers with endowment mortgages, however, get the same tax relief throughout the life of the loan because the capital owed does not reduce.

For basic-rate taxpayers, the argument could however be influenced by the borrower's age. Younger borrowers have a better chance of a 30- or 40-year mortgage, but borrowers over 35 or so may still find endowment mortgages more expensive than for 25-year-olds, because the extra insurance costs more. Borrowers in poor health or with high-risk lifestyles may also find endowment insurance expensive, but perhaps they especially need the life cover.

Borrowers with a repayment mortgage in excess of £30,000 can get a shock when the capital outstanding falls below £30,000 because the tax relief begins to shrink and the repayments rise, even under the constant net repayment system described in Chapter 3. Endowment mortgages of over £30,000 retain the maximum tax relief until they mature, and are therefore more suitable for borrowers wanting a 'limited' loan

– that is, a loan in excess of that amount.

But running costs are not the only criterion. The main attraction of a repayment mortgage is that the borrower who sells a house and pays off the mortgage can realise a cash profit (though a handful of lenders still ask for three months' interest on mortgages paid off early) and can try to retain some of that cash when buying his or her next home.

A borrower with an endowment mortgage cannot get hold of the capital built up within the policy when he or she moves house, except by surrendering the policy. While some insurance companies may pitch surrender values on the low side to discourage surrender, initial expenses have to be allowed for and borrowers who are forced for one reason or another to surrender a policy may not even get their contributions back in full if the policy has been running for less than four or five years.

If interest rates rise steeply and the cost of monthly payments escalates, most borrowers with a repayment mortgage can ask to reduce their capital repayments or pay interest only and extend the life of the mortgage. Borrowers with an endowment mortgage can often extend the term but would normally, like those with repayment mortgages, need to continue paying the interest in full.

Endowment mortgages are attractive when interest rates are low but less so if interest rates stay high for a long period. Higher-rate taxpayers get more tax relief, however, so the extra interest is less of a burden to them and the tax-free lump sum on maturity is more attractive.

Last but not least, an endowment mortgage could just possibly fail even to pay the mortgage in full if economic conditions became so bad that insurance companies could not manage to declare sufficient bonuses.

On balance, older borrowers and those with health problems might find a repayment mortgage cheaper if their dependents do not need the life insurance protection. People who expect to emigrate or to be posted abroad, and those who want to take out some of the profits whenever they move, will also find a repayment mortgage more convenient.

But younger borrowers with good prospects will tend to do

better with an endowment policy. Endowments will look more attractive if interest rates come down over the next decade or so. Borrowers who already are or expect to become higher-rate taxpayers will also find an endowment an advantage. A long period of prosperity for investments will also favour endowment mortgage holders and their tax-free terminal bonuses. Anyone with an endowment mortgage policy taken out before March 1984 should certainly hold on to it even when they move, because the premiums on endowment policies which were started before that date still qualify for tax relief.

Unit-linked endowment mortgages share the same pros and cons as ordinary endowment mortgages. They offer even bigger potential rewards if stock markets continue to go up because the bulk of the premiums are invested in stocks and shares and the profits go to the borrower. But there is potentially more risk of large swings in the value of the units. Units which have performed badly may also be less easy to transfer if borrowers want to change from one lender to another when moving house or remortgaging an existing property.

Pension mortgages are potentially even more tax-efficient, although they are still less flexible. A borrower with a pension mortgage can keep the pension plan going when moving house, but once the plan has started he or she cannot get back any capital until retirement.

Some commentators also worry that pension mortgages may tempt borrowers to neglect their real pension needs. Employees are now able to opt out of occupational schemes, join a portable pension scheme and take out a pension mortgage. The majority of company pension schemes are based on the employee's final salary, providing a tax-free lump sum and/or an element of continuing income. Switching from a pension based on final salary to one which depends on how well the contributions have been invested could be something of a gamble, especially as the proceeds of the policy must pay off the mortgage before any actual pension can be considered.

A proper assessment of individual financial planning needs is often best provided by consultation with an Independent Financial Adviser.

Whose policy?

The main attraction of an endowment mortgage is the prospect of a juicy tax-free bonus as well as just paying off the mortgage at the end of the day. With many insurance companies dangling the prospect of a substantial tax-free sum almost as big as the original mortgage loan, choosing the right insurance company is much more important than choosing the right bank or building society, or shaving a quarter point off the rate of interest on the mortgage loan itself. The best endowment insurance policy taken out in the early 1960s was worth almost exactly double the value of the worst performer when the policies matured in the late 1980s.

Track records

Track records for the profits made and bonuses paid by different insurance companies on the endowment policies they offer are now increasingly important. They are important not only to encourage the borrower but also to satisfy the lenders, who package their mortgages with endowment policies from a particular insurance company, that they are offering a product which will stand up to scrutiny and the competition.

It does not mean that the choice will now be easy. Past performance is not a guarantee for the future.

Choosing the best insurance policy will therefore always be a bit of a speculation. Past performance is the best guide anyone can hope for. Each year the magazine *Money Management* produces a list of best performers over the previous year. There are no consistent winners but the same few names tend to recur at frequent intervals.

The 'Value' column in Tables 16 and 17 shows the actual maturity value in pounds, payable on 1 February 1987, of endowment policies originally taken out by a male aged 29 at the start of the policy, paying £30 a month inclusive of policy fees (ie £3,600 over ten years, or £9,000 over 25 years). The final column shows the percentage of the maturity value which was guaranteed by cumulative bonuses. The remainder is terminal bonus, declared when the policy matured.

Table 16
Top six 10-year endowment policies

	1984	1985	1986	1987	Value (£)	Guaranteed (%)
1	Ecclesiastical	Scottish Amicable	Standard Life	Standard Life	9,024	59
2	Equitable Life	Standard Life	Scottish Amicable	Scottish Widows'	8,977	60
3	Standard Life	Norwich Union	Scottish Widows'	Clerical Medical	8,943	59
4	Norwich Union	Scottish Widows'	Equitable Life	Friends' Provident	8,577	66
5	Scottish Widows'	Ecclesiastical	Clerical Medical	Norwich Union	8,431	70
6	Refuge Assurance	Tunbridge Wells	Tunbridge Wells	Equitable Life	8,353	65

Source *Money Management*, May 1987

Table 17
Top six 25-year endowment policies

	1984	1985	1986	1987	Value (£)	Guaranteed (%)
1	Standard Life	Scottish Amicable	Standard Life	Standard Life	52,608	42
2	Clerical Medical	Standard Life	Clerical Medical	Scottish Amicable	49,424	46
3	Scottish Amicable	Clerical Medical	Scottish Amicable	Scottish Widows'	49,113	48
4	Ecclesiastical	Norwich Union	Scottish Widows'	Scottish Life	48,250	45
5	Equity & Law	Scottish Widows'	Norwich Union	Clerical Medical	48,225	59
6	Norwich Union	Friends' Provident	Scottish Life	Norwich Union	48,198	68

Bonus policy

The value of the policy when it matures is the most important consideration for most borrowers with an endowment mortgage. But prudent borrowers will also be interested in the way bonuses build up. Some insurance companies are cautious in adding guaranteed annual bonuses, and concentrate much more on a large terminal bonus, which does not have to be added until the policy matures. Other insurers offer larger guaranteed bonuses, leaving smaller bonuses to be added when the policy matures. Life offices with a smaller proportion of terminal bonus provide more certainty of the final payout as maturity approaches.

Although the difference is academic for borrowers whose policies run to maturity, anyone who needs to surrender the policy before it matures will do better with a policy which offers larger guaranteed annual bonuses. According to *Money Management*, the ten best policies maturing in 1987 showed consistently good performances, but terminal bonuses accounted for 60 per cent of the total paid out by Standard Life and over 50 per cent of the pay-out from Scottish Life, Scottish Amicable and Scottish Widows'. At the other end of the scale, terminal bonuses made up just over 30 per cent of the total paid by Norwich Union. Commercial Union, which did not quite make the top ten, paid less than 20 per cent of the total as terminal bonuses.

Surrender values

Borrowers who have to cash in an endowment policy early do not always receive an allowance for terminal bonus and may not even receive the full amount of premiums they have paid – partly because insurance companies want to discourage policyholders from taking money away early, and partly because they do have to cover their administrative costs, the commission they paid the agent who sold the policy, and the costs of realizing investments to repay the premiums. But some are more generous than others in the surrender values they pay on policies cashed in early. *Money Management* in 1987 rated Standard Life, Norwich Union and London Life the three best

Table 18
Surrender values of 25-year endowment policies

After 2 years Company	Value (£)	After 5 years Company	Value (£)	After 12 years Company	Value (£)
1 Equitable	739	General Accident	1,970	Norwich Union	9,165
2 London Life	612	London Life	1,966	Standard Life	8,732
3 LAS	596	Nat. Mutual Life	1,897	Sun Alliance	8,591
4 Standard Life	549	Scottish Mutual	1,876	Scottish Amicable	7,852
5 Equity & Law	546	Standard Life	1,875	Scottish Provident	7,844
6 Scot. Widows'	545	Equitable	1,858	National Prov.	7,402

Figures are for a male aged 29 at the start of the policy, paying £30 a month gross premium. The premiums paid therefore total £720 after 2 years, £1800 after 5 years and £4,320 after 12 years.
Source *Money Management*, May 1986

companies for good surrender values on 25-year endowment policies. Norwich Union itself claims that its current surrender value on a 25-year policy cashed in after 12 years is 50 per cent above the average.

Unit-linked or pension mortgages

There are well over 100 unit trust managers and over 1,000 unit trusts on the market, many of which provide investment vehicles for unit-linked policies. Their performance varies widely from year to year – much more widely than the value of endowment policies. Many trusts have been set up within the last year or two, and very few have been around for more than ten years. The value of unit trusts is monitored by magazines such as *Money Management*, and their performance in recent years has been remarkable. But the gains looked much less impressive after the stock markets crashed in October 1987 – the Australian stock market in particular suffered badly.

Most pension mortgages are with-profits rather than unit-linked and their performance is more closely related to endowment insurance policy performance than to unit-linked policies.

Selling the best

Banks and building societies have been forced to choose whether they will act as independent agents for other companies' products or sell their own packages. Abbey National has chosen to sell Friends' Provident policies and the Chelsea has linked up with Guardian Royal Exchange. By the beginning of 1988, two dozen other societies had also decided to act as representatives of a single insurance company. Other building societies have chosen to act as independent agents.

Lenders who choose to remain independent advisers keep a panel of insurance companies whose policies they regard as safe and profitable. They may have ten or a dozen different insurance companies on their panel, and offer borrowers one or other of their policies. The building society earns a commission, normally about 60 per cent of the first year's premium, from the insurance company whose 25-year policy is chosen to go with the mortgage.

The precise choice of which insurance policy to package with the endowment mortgage has always been informal in the past – it has often been left to the branch manager to decide which ones to suggest. The borrower is free to demand a different company, but in the past has normally accepted the building society's suggestion without question.

That may well change, however, as the new legislation takes effect and building societies may well be forced to tell the borrower precisely why they are recommending a particular insurance company and also (if asked) precisely how much commission they are earning. Some astute borrowers may well be tempted to demand a share of the building society's commission, although the building society might be tempted in return to charge for its advice.

Foreign banks that have entered the mortgage market and the new mortgage companies have few outlets or salesmen of their own. They do not qualify as intermediaries, and need to retain links with a wide range of insurance companies and brokers acting as a channel for their mortgages.

The clearing banks – Barclays, National Westminster, Lloyds, Midland, the TSB, the Royal Bank of Scotland, the

Bank of Scotland, the Co-operative and the Yorkshire – faced a much harder choice because they had the branches and the customers which would allow them to offer a wide choice of policies. They also keep a panel of insurance companies to provide backing for the endowment mortgages which the banks offer. But they have also developed their own in-house unit trust management facilities, which they would not be allowed to recommend to customers if they decided to register as independent agents.

Some of the banks considered setting up separate subsidiaries to market their own products, but most of them have now chosen to act as principals and sell mortgage packages complete with finance and endowment insurance policies of their own choice, and not to act as independents. National Westminster, alone of the big clearing banks, has sold its unit trust management business and chosen to become an independent adviser, offering borrowers a free choice of policies to go with its mortgages.

The insurance industry has also divided on the issue. Those companies which employ their own sales-force to sell their own insurance policies and unit trusts direct to the public – including the Prudential, the Pearl and the newer companies like Allied Dunbar and Save & Prosper – have also decided to go on selling their own packages and not to become independent advisers.

Many insurance companies do not employ their own sales-force, and a group of 14 insurance companies, led by the Norwich Union and a number of the old-established Scottish-based companies, took the lead in organizing CAMIFA, a campaign to persuade thousands of independent brokers and financial advisers around the country to stay independent and not to sign up as tied agents for one or other of the big groups.

CAMIFA will also be working to make the public aware of the benefits of independent financial advice.

The changes taking place have all been triggered by the desire to promote competition while protecting the consumer. There is no doubt that they are increasing both competition and choice for the borrower, bringing charges further out into the open and pointing the finger of publicity at the differences in the way endowment insurance policies marketed by different companies have performed. Independent advisers also have to reveal how much commission they earn, if asked.

How long a mortgage?

Most borrowers instinctively try to borrow as much as possible, as cheaply as possible and for as long a period as possible. The standard mortgage is meant to be paid back in 25 years, but 30-year and 35-year mortgages are available, and a handful of specialist lenders have been advertising mortgages which can be paid back over as long as 40 years. The longer the mortgage lasts, the smaller the capital repayments on a repayment mortgage and the smaller the annual premiums on an endowment required, each year, and so the more the ambitious borrower can afford to borrow at the start.

A borrower who can afford to pay £150 a month could borrow £18,350 if it has to be repaid over 20 years. But the same payment would service a mortgage of £20,065 over 25 years and £21,258 over 30 years. But the cost of repaying the smaller loan over 20 years mounts up to not quite £36,000, the middle-sized loan over 25 years grows to a total cost of almost £45,000 and the larger loan over 30 years amounts to a total payment of nearly £54,000, assuming a gross mortgage rate of 10 per cent and tax relief at 25p in the pound.

With an endowment mortgage there is less incentive to go for a long mortgage because (assuming interest rates stay unchanged) the total amount of interest paid each year is the same, regardless of how long the mortgage is – although the annual insurance premiums will be slightly lower if the payments are spread over a longer period.

Borrowers who are anxious to get as high up the housing ladder as possible in one step, and who are sure that house prices will go on rising, will want to take out as long a mortgage as they can, in order to borrow more to start with. Normally the lenders will have no objection, provided the borrower's health and prospects are good. But the annual endowment premium rises steadily with the borrower's age at the start of the policy, if that age is much over 35.

Experience has shown that inflation quickly reduces the real burden of a mortgage, however, and most lenders are now quite happy to offer mortgages which borrowers will still be paying back after they reach normal retirement age.

But if inflation stays under control, the real burden of a mortgage will not melt away as rapidly in the future as it did in the past 20 years, and if interest rates remain above inflation, taking out an extended mortgage will not be such obvious good sense as it was in the 1960s and 1970s. It depends on the level of real interest rates and whether housing stays the best long-term investment.

Early repayment

The same arguments apply to the question of whether to pay off a mortgage early. Most of the larger building societies no longer charge a fee to borrowers who want to redeem their mortgage early. But some societies, mainly the smaller ones, do still charge a fee, usually the equivalent of three months' interest. Most of the British banks allow early repayment without penalty, although the Bank of Scotland is an exception. A number of insurance companies – including Guardian Royal Exchange, Equity & Law, Canada Life and Royal London – either charge a fee or require three months' notice or interest in lieu. But there are no penalties for accelerating repayments and keeping only a token loan going, and in any case the penalties have never been a serious deterrent to paying off a mortgage.

But paying off an endowment mortgage in the early years is often unwise, because the surrender value of the endowment policy will not be very high. Borrowers who need to pay off the mortgage are often best advised to try to maintain the policy as an investment. Choosing whether to pay a repayment mortgage off early is an investment decision. During the 1970s, no one would have even considered it. Inflation was steadily reducing the value of money, and the real burden of a mortgage was shrinking markedly year by year. Even the high rates of interest made no difference: after tax relief, mortgages were very cheap indeed – certainly the cheapest form of borrowing available – and borrowers held on to mortgages as a matter of course.

Now that inflation has diminished and interest rates are higher than inflation, the argument is no longer quite so clear-cut. In particular, pensioners who receive a lump sum as well as a pension when they retire are often tempted to pay off any mortgage they may still have on their home. With mortgage interest at around 10 per cent and inflation at 4 or 5 per cent, having a mortgage now carries a real cost, even after tax relief on the interest. The decision to keep it going or pay it off depends on what else the borrower might do with the money that would be used.

A £10,000 mortgage at 10 per cent gross interest is costing a basic-rate taxpayer only 7.5 per cent net of tax. By paying it off, he or she can save £750 a year. If instead that £10,000 is invested at an interest rate of 8 per cent net of tax, it will earn £800 a year. Using capital to pay off the mortgage early would not really be worthwhile, however, especially if the lender charges a penalty. It is certainly not worthwhile selling shares to pay off a mortgage if the stock market is rising strongly.

If a borrower has capital which is invested in National Savings Certificates (earning, say, 7 per cent tax free) it is theoretically worthwhile to cash them in and pay off the mortgage. But if you think interest rates are coming down, and the mortgage might soon cost only 5 per cent net of tax, it would make no sense to cash in savings certificates and lose the guaranteed tax-free return on them over the next five years. Higher-rate taxpayers would be even less well advised to sell tax-free savings certificates. A mortgage of less than £30,000 costs a top-rate taxpayer only 60 per cent of the quoted interest rate after tax relief, and considerably less than the borrower could earn on tax-free investments like savings certificates.

Using a broker (or estate agent)

The majority of borrowers get a mortgage that suits their needs, at a reasonable cost and in absolute security, from their local building society or bank, without ever needing to shop around. There is no real need for them to go to a broker or financial adviser, or to take a mortgage and endowment policy package from the estate agent who sells them the house.

But there is no harm in finding out what these other sources of finance have to offer, provided you feel able to say no if the interest rate seems expensive or the endowment policy offered does not come from an insurance company with a good track record. Those intermediaries who have registered with FIMBRA as independent financial advisers are required under The Financial Services Act to provide 'best advice' concerning the insurance company they recommend. Mortgage brokers earn most of their money as commission for providing advice on the companies whose products they include in a mortgage package. Estate agents also get commission on the endowment policies they help to sell. Brokers and agents normally charge the borrower a fee only if they arrange a repayment mortgage or a remortgage which does not require an additional endowment policy because they will not be providing a package on which they can earn any commission. The usual charge ranges from 0.5 per cent to one per cent. On a top-up loan the broker may earn commission on any new policy required and also charge a fee for making part use of existing policies.

A straightforward endowment or pension mortgage arranged through a broker or estate agent should not cost the borrower any more than it would from a bank or building society or from a lender advertising in a newspaper or magazine. The lender saves on advertising and administration what he pays out in commission to the broker who acts as the link with the public. Some of these packages are available only through a broker.

But borrowers who use a broker should check whose endowment policy will be packaged with the loan. Many small brokers, and estate agents who also act as brokers, are not independent and in practice sell the financial packages provided by only one supplier. Ask whether or not they are independent and members of FIMBRA. Borrowers who are looking for an endowment, a unit-linked or a pension mortgage should make sure that they are dealing with a genuinely independent broker, ask for advice regarding a choice of endowment policies, and then check the latest performance record of the policies the broker offers in a magazine such as *Money Management*.

An independent broker may sometimes have been tempted to suggest a de luxe mortgage package equipped with many optional extras, or to suggest additional insurance or savings plans which were nothing to do with the mortgage but on which he could earn more commission. But under the new legal rules he is duty-bound to provide his client with the investment which is best suited to the borrower's particular needs. The borrower is under no obligation to accept.

It is borrowers with special requirements who stand to gain most from consulting a broker – including higher-rate tax-payers, anyone who wants to borrow more than conventional lenders such as building societies currently think is prudent, those who want to buy an unusual type of home, anyone who depends heavily on bonuses, commission and other irregular earnings, anyone in a risky kind of job and self-employed people who are thinking about a pension scheme.

A broker might well have the contacts needed to find a lender willing to give a mortgage where others would not do so. He might well know a lender that is anxious to get into the mortgage market or increase its market share, and is therefore willing to lend more, for longer or shorter than the normal period, and to consider special types of property which some lenders are reluctant to lend on – including freehold flats, leasehold properties with only a short lease remaining, proper-ties with a sitting tenant and only part vacant possession, and timber-frame homes or thatched cottages. A broker may be able to provide a more flexible package, or to combine the mortgage with an investment, insurance, pension or tax avoidance plan. Brokers may be the best source of top-up loans.

As the choice of mortgage plans becomes increasingly varied, brokers expect more demand for their services.

Are they safe?

This ought to be the first question borrowers ask when choos-ing a mortgage. It is usually the last, or it is never asked at all because lenders have an enviable record in the last half-century in making mortgage loans and administering them. A handful of building societies have ceased trading as a result of fraud, incompetence or simply over-reaching themselves and failing to attract and hold on to the savings they need to finance their mortgage lending. But in these cases the business has been taken over (usually by another, larger society) and no borrower has lost money as a result.

In the past, the Building Societies Association acted as an unofficial safety net, ensuring that one or other of its members mounted a rescue operation. But protection for savers and borrowers is now organized officially by the Building Societies Commission, with the former Chief Registrar of Friendly Societies as its first chairman.

A number of small banks went bust during the secondary banking crisis in 1973–74, and their commercial creditors and shareholders suffered financial losses. But their small investors and their borrowers were all fully protected by arrangements put together by the Bank of England. That role has now been taken over by a fund paid for by the entire banking system.

Foreign banks are also all now licensed by the Bank of England before they can open their doors for business in Britain, and their banking customers are protected by an unofficial mutual guarantee system operated by the central banks of all the countries with banks in this country.

The insurance companies are monitored by the Department of Trade, and are all obliged to publish their accounts to show that they are trading prudently, even if not profitably, and that they have reserves in hand to meet all their obligations. The newly established mortgage companies are either public companies owned by shareholders who absorb the first losses if they go out of business, or they are owned by groups of large companies which are themselves responsible if the mortgage company fails.

Mortgage brokers and financial advisers who act as independent agents in putting borrowers and lenders in touch with each other are all obliged by law to be members of FIMBRA, the Financial Intermediaries, Managers and Brokers Regulatory Association. FIMBRA lays down rules for keeping clients' money separate from the firm's own cash, monitors the firm's performance and compensates small customers out of a central fund if losses arise from the incompetence or fraudulence of the firm or its employees.

12
Special schemes and half-way houses

The mortgage market has been very successful in helping a majority of the population to buy homes of their own in the past four decades. But it has also been the victim of its own success, certainly in southern England. The sheer demand for home ownership and the weight of money put in buyers' hands by building societies, banks and the new generation of lenders has helped to force up property values and has priced ordinary homes out of the reach of most people who are not yet home owners.

Getting on to the first rung of the housing ladder is especially difficult for young couples who have already started families and no longer have the benefit of two incomes to finance a mortgage. Single-parent families find mortgages difficult if not impossible to finance while making ends meet on low incomes.

Older people who failed to see the financial advantages of buying a home of their own, or could not afford it while their families were growing up, may also feel they have missed the boat. And retired people who no longer have an earned income and live on state and company pensions also find the prospect of trying to buy a home of their own financially daunting. Widows and widowers who have not bought property at some time in the past are the worst placed of all.

Not everyone wants to buy a conventional home with a conventional mortgage, and a substantial minority could not in any case afford to buy property at current prices. Young single people leaving home often do not want a house or flat of their own even if they can afford it, and the conventional mortgage market offers them little or nothing either, especially in London and south-east England. But the problem of fitting housing supplies to housing needs has become more acute everywhere in the country.

Builders have recognized the problems the young, the single and the old have in buying suitable homes of their own by cutting down the numbers of detached and three-bedroomed semi-detached homes being built in the last decade or so, and building many more homes to suit these groups – one- and two-bedroomed houses and flats, which also have the advantage of being cheaper to build and buy. Building societies and banks have also produced schemes to help buyers at both ends of the age range.

Special schemes for the young

Special schemes for young people include long-term mortgages with payments spread over anything from 26 to 40 years, backed by special low-cost endowment policies. Working Life Mortgages from the Halifax for example guarantee long-term mortgages on a first home and the promise of further mortgages on subsequent homes.

Low-start mortgages with reduced payments and built-in life insurance for the first few years are also offered by a growing number of lenders. In many cases they are available in conjunction with the government's Homeloan scheme, which gives a £110 cash grant and an interest-free loan of £600 for five years to couples who have saved the same amount themselves over the previous two years.

Maturity mortgages

Some lenders also offer interest-only mortgages to older people to help them buy suitable homes for retirement. Several lenders offer interest-only schemes to borrowers aged 50 or more, and at least one scheme starts at 45. But they all assume the borrower already has savings or capital tied up in an existing home. A typical scheme would lend up to 60 per cent of the value or the purchase price, whichever is the lower, and borrowers pay only the interest. The loan itself is repaid only when the owner, or the last survivor in the case of a couple, has died and the property has been sold. The balance of the property price, including all the increase in value since the mortgage was taken out, goes to the estate. In some cases the Department of Health and Social Security will also help retired people to pay the interest on special mortgage loans.

Elderly people can also take out mortgage loans on their own existing property to buy an annuity, which is enough to pay the interest on the mortgage and also to provide extra income in retirement. The arrangement lasts as long as the borrower or surviving spouse lives. After that the loan is paid off out of the value of the estate. The best-known scheme is run by Allied Dunbar Provident, but the Halifax and Abbey National building societies also offer schemes.

These loans are usually available only to people aged 70 or more, and subject to a minimum of about £15,000 and a maximum of £30,000. Annuity schemes do not however release any capital for elderly people to spend. Home Reversions offers to buy the homes of elderly people at half price, and allow them to live rent-free until they die.

Retirement homes

A growing array of special schemes are also available to elderly and retired people, many of whom find themselves living in family homes which are now too large and too expensive to maintain. In the last few years, an army of builders have developed special housing schemes for the elderly, building sheltered accommodation for rent or for sale. Sheltered housing schemes usually incorporate resident wardens, security devices and group facilities specially designed for old people. Service charges can however be quite high.

Housing associations

Special schemes also exist to help ordinary borrowers of any age who cannot afford a conventional mortgage. Housing associations have helped to provide an estimated 500,000 homes for people who could not afford to step straight on to the housing ladder. They are non-profitmaking groups, usually run by charities or voluntary trusts, which buy land and employ contractors to build groups of houses or blocks of flats, or buy and renovate older properties usually owned by private landlords in inner-city areas. The homes are rented to their occupants. Some associations specialize in providing homes for people for whom the housing market does not normally cater – including young single people, the elderly and disabled people – but many provide housing for a full range of people, most of whom are on waiting-lists for council housing.

Since 1980, tenants of housing associations not run by charities have had the right to buy the freeholds at prices below market values on similar terms to those enjoyed by council tenants, financed by individual mortgages from building societies or banks. Since 1974, all housing associations have been supervised by the Housing Corporation, a statutory body which provides around £700 million a year in grants to the 2,600 registered housing associations around the country. In 1987 the government allowed housing associations to apply for loans from banks and building societies as well as the Housing Corporation. Housing associations are also now being encouraged to take over the administration of local authority housing.

Shared-ownership schemes

Since the mid-1970s, housing associations have also been organizing shared-ownership schemes to develop and build groups of houses or flats, or buy and convert existing properties. Members of the schemes are able to buy part of the value of their homes, usually 25 per cent, 50 per cent or 75 per cent at a time, and pay rent on the remainder until they are ready and able to buy the whole lease.

Shared-ownership schemes have been run either by housing associations or by local authorities. But the 1986 Building Societies Act now allows societies to act as middlemen, providing finance, employing contractors and administering the schemes as well as providing mortgages for the tenants to start buying their shares. One of the first to start was the

Woolwich, building 200 homes in six different places, to be sold on 100 per cent mortgages, with the buyer paying only 70 per cent of the interest due in return for giving the Woolwich 30 per cent of any eventual capital profit.

Building societies also have the right to make loans to individual property buyers at reduced interest rates in return for a share of the profit when they sell. Nationwide Anglia set up a Partnership Mortgage scheme to lend money at two-thirds the normal interest rates to approved employees of the National Health Service wanting to buy property in Greater London; in return, the Society expects half the profit, up to a maximum of 15 per cent a year, to be paid only when the property is sold or the mortgage matures. Similar schemes for other areas and other social groups, such as teachers, are planned. The Halifax, the Woolwich and the Alliance & Leicester also have shared-ownership schemes.

Self-build schemes

Building societies also now have the right to provide finance for self-build groups, usually in co-operation with local authorities. Most self-build groups enlist the services of craftsmen – especially builders, plumbers, carpenters and electricians – drawn mainly from local housing waiting-lists, who agree to contribute time and labour to help build a group of homes. A building society will normally provide finance to pay for land and materials and for specialized labour. Members draw lots to allocate the homes as they are finished, but all members pay rent to the group until all the homes are ready. They are then eligible to apply for mortgage loans from the building society of their own choice.

Self-build housing schemes may take anything from a year to two years to complete a project, with the members working mostly part time. But the finished project usually costs only about two-thirds of the market value of the property, bringing a home and a mortgage within reach of families who otherwise might not be able to afford it.

Urban renewal

Building societies have also become involved in urban renewal schemes, helping to finance the renovation for sale of older houses in inner-city areas, originally owned by private landlords. Most of these houses lacked basic amenities including bathrooms and inside lavatories, and had become run down and neglected as a result of rent control. Many similar houses were pulled down during the massive slum clearance programmes in the 1950s and 1960s, and replaced by tower blocks.

The original schemes to restore rather than demolish them were sponsored by local architects or action groups and financed by a number of pioneering building societies, especially the National & Provincial building society based in Bradford. But the riots in Brixton and Toxteth and other deprived inner-city areas focused attention on the need for more schemes to try to reverse inner-city decay and improve the quality of inner-city housing. The initiatives set in motion in 1982 by Mr Michael Heseltine as Minister of the Environment have involved a much larger number of societies in urban renewal schemes in inner-city areas, especially in the north of England. But so far they have only begun to scratch the surface of the problem of helping inner cities share in the prosperity which owner-occupation has brought to the suburbs.

Index